Superconscious Meditation

Pandit Usharbudh Arya, Ph.D.

Himalayan International Institute

Honesdale, Pennsylvania

ISBN: 0-89389-035-9

Copyright 1978

HIMALAYAN INTERNATIONAL INSTITUTE
RD 1 Honesdale, Pennsylvania 18431

First Edition 1974
Second Edition 1977

Contents

Preface

The history of mankind is the history of the human mind. All man's tools, dwellings and weapons; all the means of his comfort and discomfort have arisen from his will and knowledge which produce action; and yet in his long march through many errors and corrections, there is one error that the majority of human persons have not yet corrected. They view their material environment as the prime factor in their development. This is because the senses open outwards and gather their data from the surroundings. They are not equipped to test or to infer their own existence, let alone the existence of an inward world finer than the senses. There is one thing that the eyes do not see: the eyes. The mind is not trained to know the self.

Even though the above is true of most human beings, there have been a few minds of finer sensitivity who have looked at themselves and made the discovery of the true Self their life's pursuit. It would be wrong to say that these men have always withdrawn physically from their social and material environment, or that they have tried to escape from the unbearable pains which the human condition often enforces upon the body and mind.

The great rishis of ancient India, the prophets of the Old Testament, the early seers of Greece were all people involved with their daily family lives. But there was a spiritual center to their being from which they derived the tranquil light that helped them shape the vision of a different humanity.

One may look for things with the help of a light, but where is the light with which one may search for the inner light? Which is the eye wherewith one may see the eye itself? That state of consciousness in which I knows I is called meditation. In these pages we want to present the tradition of Superconscious Meditation, which is the true union of the self with Self. Superconscious Meditation is the science by which a person may come to know his own self and the Self of all.

Introduction

The method of Superconscious Meditation is a highly systematic and scientific one which leads the student from his gross level of awareness to the highest and most subtle state of consciousness.

This method is not a mere technique of relaxation but a method which makes the student aware of the whole philosophy of life and the knowledge of the fourth state which is beyond waking, dreaming, and sleeping. Ordinarily, all living creatures remain only aware of the three states of mind—waking, dreaming and sleeping. With the help of Superconscious Meditation, however, one can attain the fourth state which is called *turiya*.

Meditation is an inward way of fathoming all the levels of consiousness, from where consciousness flows on various degrees and grades. It is a tradition of the ancient sages of the Vedic period which does not oppose modern science.

This book will primarily serve the purpose of understanding the whole process of meditation with the complete philosophy of life. Those who are prepared to tread the ancient path of sages will find this book very useful.

Dr. Usharbudh Arya has systematically described this method in *Superconscious Meditation.* I appreciate his sincere efforts in writing this book. Dr. Arya follows this ancient path of sages and practices the discipline of meditation faithfully.

Swami Rama

I
The Tradition

There is a story in the *Upanishads*.

Once upon a time, God the Progenitor (Prajapati) had two groups of children, gods (*devas*) and demons (*asuras*), who were fighting among themselves for the mastery of the three worlds. Suddenly they heard an announcement. Prajapati declared: "There is a self, free of all sins, without death or decay, devoid of hunger and thirst, with no grief or sorrow, ever inclined towards truth, resolved upon truth, fully knowing all things. He who knows this self soon becomes the master of the three worlds." Upon hearing this declaration, the two sides dispatched emissaries who approached Prajapati and inquired of him about this secret concerning the self, by knowing which one may become a master of the three worlds. Now the name of the representative of the devas was Indra, the masterful soul; the demons were represented by Virochana, the glamorous one. They approached Prajapati and asked the secret of the self. Prajapati, as the tradition of the ancients goes, ordered them to go through a process of austerities and practices for a period of thirty-six years. After the thirty-six years were over, they reminded him of his promise to tell them the secret of the self. Prajapati said, "Well, shave yourselves, wash yourselves, eat and drink, be filled, look your handsome selves . . . now go and see yourselves reflected in a pool of water. Are you not handsome? Do you have any sorrow? Are you hungry? Thirsty?" And they said, "No, we are completely satisfied." They were told, "Well, you now know of the self."

Quite satisfied, both of them proceeded back to their respective camps. Virochana, the glamorous one, returned to his clan, and declared this body to be the true self. Love it, worship it, anoint it, center all your activities and pursuits around the comforts and desires of the body. Adore it, and make it adorable and you know the self. Says the text, even to this day, the clan of the demons anoint and adorn a dead body hoping to preserve it as man's true self. But Indra, the masterful soul, was somewhat more inquisitive and turned back halfway home, and questioned Prajapati further.   Prajapati ordered him through another period of thirty-six years of austerities, at the end of which he was advised that indeed what he experienced of the body during the wakeful state was not the true self. The true self is experienced in the dream state when even a hungry man may feel filled, even an old man may see himself young. This time again, Indra started out but returned from halfway and said to Prajapati that his statement concerning the experience of self during the dream state did not hold true according to Prajapati's own definition of the true nature of the self; because often in a dream, even a king may feel great grief, and there is certainly a world of illusion and not right knowledge and true resolves. Prajapati completely agreed and ordered him through another period of thirty-six years of meditative practice, at the end of which he was told that the sleep state was the true consciousness of self, for in sleep there is no hunger, no thirst, no grief, no sorrow. This time Indra thought that he had indeed discovered the true self, but as he was walking back to his people he reflected: in the sleep state there is no consciousness, there is no awareness, there is all negation; even though there is no hunger, thirst or grief, there is no inclination towards a resolve of truth. He came back to the guru, who agreed that the sleep state also was not an experience of true consciousness of the self. Five more years and it was then that Indra, after a total of one hundred and thirteen years of practice, finally learned to transcend the limited states of wakefulness, dreaming and sleep.

We ordinarily experience only these three states of consciousness because of the way our senses and the mind have been educated and trained from our very childhood.

We have two types of senses: active and cognitive. With the active senses, such as hands, feet, generative organs, speech and so forth, we proceed out towards other objects and persons. We seldom pause to look exactly from where within ourselves this proceeding originates. We are not aware of some focal point of consciousness in ourselves from where the first command within the depths of the mind goes out to the hand to

move.   So also with our cognitive senses, the senses of
experience. Through these senses we absorb the information from without; we see, hear, smell, taste and touch.
Again we do not pause to look for a center to which
each bit of information goes and where it is stored.   In
other words, we do not observe the formation of our own
subconscious mind; it grows and grows like a rubbish
heap in the backyard and spreads its odors to the entire
neighborhood.

What happens to a view when the eyes have seen it?
Look at the wall of your room for half a minute.   It
appears as if it were the continuity of a single experience.
But that is an illusion, just like looking at a movie. From
micro-instant to micro-instant the eyes are receiving the
light reflected from the wall.   But what happens after you
have seen it?   Where is that experience stored? A psychologist may form many theories and may analyze others'
behavior in the light of those theories, and yet he has
seldom paused to observe himself observing the objects
in the wakeful state or their impressions being left on his
mind.

Wakefulness, then, is the interaction of the conscious mind through the senses with the objective world.
The dream state is the mind chewing its own cud and sleep
is a state in which the mind is absorbed in the comtempla-
tion of archetypal negation.   Imagine a room in which a
monkey is tied to a rope, a room with windows and doors
open.   The rope is long enough for the monkey to jump
in and out of the windows but the rope prevents him from
escaping altogether.   He picks up random objects from the

room and flings them out of the windows. This is called action. He also picks up random objects from outside and flings them into the room. This is called experience. Action and experience are the two sides of the same coin. However, it is unfortunate that we seldom act, and most often only react to experiences. This is called wakefulness. Now shut the doors and the windows, but the monkey is still awake. He shatters the plates against the inside walls and mixes up all the different objects within the room. This is the state of dream and fantasies.

The ancient yoga psychologists insistently differentiated between dream and sleep states. This distinction is now borne out in the scientific experiments with biofeedback, as it has been observed that the brain emits beta waves both in wakefulness and dream states and delta waves in deep sleep. The monkey called the mind tires of its plate-smashing and lies down to rest. This is called the sleep state.

Meditation is the fourth state. Ask someone in meditation, "Are you awake?" and the answer is "no." "Are you asleep?" Still "no." The state of meditation has nothing in common with the first three. In these three states, the consciousness associates itself with the idea of otherness; with the dichotomies of I and Thou, I and This. Thou and This are prominent, and the "I" in relation to them is a mere false ego. Meditation is the life-force aware of itself, and of no other objects of experience nor of conscious memories; nor subconscious dreaming and fantasizing memories of those experiences; nor of sleeping negation of the objects, experiences and memories.

It is not a state in which time, space and sequence play any part. Many have tried to define it, but all have failed; we are forced to invent words, terms, and definitions; we are compelled to write these sentences but we are not saying what the reader is comprehending.

One might say that it is all a sleight of hand, the trickery of a mind that does not know how to define. What is the proof that such a state exists? Who has tested it? What are your control groups and your data? Now, our answer is that this is *beyond* the rational process; not irrational but *supra-rational*. Rationality is only a small faculty, among others, of consciousness, and the individual parts cannot be demonstrated in the world of objects. But this should not lead us to a fallacious conclusion that its experience cannot be tried by the individual or that the state itself cannot be communicated by a powerful mind, the guru, to a disciple. Quite contrary is the truth, but of that later.

Meditation has been described by its proponents as a science, and yet we are denying the validity of an objective approach for testing the claims of meditation. In this science, the scientist himself is the guinea pig, the observer is the observed. It is the eye recognizing its own gleam, its own power to see, even if an object of sight is not present. Let us try to understand this by an analogy: a flame illuminates the objects around it, but it is self-luminous. The illumination of the other objects is dependent on the flame's light—it is not the totality, but only one of the proofs of the flame's luminosity, which is independent of the objects it illuminates. Regard this flame to be the center of man's conscious personality; its consciousness is not dependent on the objects of which the mind and the senses become conscious. Unfortunately, through wrong training, we have suppressed this self-awareness of consciousness. So long as I am conscious of objects, then I know I am conscious. If I am not conscious of an object, then I must be unconscious. This faulty reasoning leads us to constant dependence on our environment and situations to which we react instead of acting independently out of the luminosity of the inner self. It is as if we were constantly sending out the sonar waves like a bat and only as they return to us do we say, "Because this wave returned to me, I must be." "Because I see, I am; because I hear, I am; because I taste, touch and smell, I am." The proponent of meditation states, "I am, therefore I think, I see, I hear."

There is no way in which one may objectively study another person, another consciousness, because the moment you attempt to do so, the other becomes the object and the nature of the subject is forgotten. Meditation is the science in which the subject seeks to know the subject, the self seeks to experience the self, without reference to other stimuli, or to any responses to those stimuli, without using other measuring rods. We say the self is the measureless measure of the self. The self is its own proof; *the states of consciousness alone are proof of the states of consciousness.*

The states of consciousness alone are proof of the states of consciousness. Some of their signs and symptoms may be measurable, but their *feel* cannot be measured by another person with any measuring device. A state of consciousness itself is non-discursive and non-verbal. It is not so much a *think* but, I repeat, a *feel*. An experience always comes as a feel, before it finds rational categories and right words to express itself. A child is born and at the moment of the birth he has no conception of language, no word for "I am," and yet he feels a non-verbal state of "I am," from which he cries or laughs or wiggles his body or focuses his eyes and without a word for milk experiences the taste of milk. By the time he finds the word *milk*, he has already forgotten the taste of the mother's milk. Does that mean that that experience, that *feel*, of milk does not exist? A thorn gets into the sole of your foot. It is first an experience and only then an interjection, a cry of pain, and a verbal description. One may write many treatises, theorizing about pain, yet neither writing nor reading all those learned tomes can give you the experience of a thorn penetrating the skin of the sole. You love and it is a feeling, non-discursive and non-verbal before your mind looks for the words and finds "I love you." As you read this, it is evident that you are awake, yet all this while you have not been repeating, "I am awake, I am awake." Wakefulness is a non-verbal experience. Your wakefulness cannot be conveyed to another. It can be proved only because another person has similar but not the same experiences. You may compare notes with others about the experiences of wakefulness, but your own wakefulness is an intensely private and individual *feel*.

Let us take another example: supposing you have

a guest born in a strange country, where the taste of sugar is not known. Now, if such a guest asks you to describe the taste of sugar, how can you do this for him? You can only ask that he should taste it himself, but if he adamantly refuses to experiment with a strange new taste, there is no way you can convince him of the desirability of the experience.

The meditative person says: try it, and take note of whatever experience comes to you; it will be a non-verbal feel to express which you will look for words and then will be in the same quandary as this writer because the experience cannot be described. Suppose again, that the beings of a distant planet experience only wakefulness and deep sleep but do not dream. If one of these beings happens to come down to the earth, is there some way in which you can describe to him the dream state and prove that it could truly exist?

Fortunately there are methods of teaching the art and science of meditation. These methods cover many aspects of life and the needs and problems of all different personalities. People come to the meditative life and practices from all different backgrounds, seeking solutions to many different problems. There are at present three types of yoga known to the West. I call these Hollywood yoga, Harvard yoga and Himalayan yoga.

The Hollywood yoga appeals to the people who aspire for a fit body, eternal youth and physical beauty. It is the aspect of yoga that appeals to the Virochana mind and this type of mind does not wish to go beyond, even though the same physical preparations are an invaluable aid and important steps to a higher meditative life.

The Harvard yoga is the aspect that appeals to a scientist who is interested in analyzing the activity of the brain, control of the nervous system, and autogenic training. This aspect concerns itself with the signs and symptoms produced by certain states of consciousness, but does not aspire to grasp the self-luminosity of the consciousness force.

This last is the highest aim of the Himalayan yogis and is called *samadhi*, the knowledge of the self that is pure Self. As one starts off from the basic physical steps on a long journey to the homeland of consciousness, one naturally comes across various *siddhis*, powers over the body, mind and external matter.

The teachers of meditation recognize that not all people take to this inquiry with the highest aim of *samadhi.* Some are interested only in physical culture, seeking youth, beauty and health. Others are looking for solutions to the emotional problems or the problems of family and social relationships. The anxiety-ridden minds produce tense nerves and create many mental and physical disorders. The various levels of training and practice help solve these problems, and there are methods to deal with each of these. No one is expected to go beyond. A master in the yoga tradition is an expert at all these different methods of solving the various problems and fulfilling the needs of each individual, according to his own aspirations. A set of practices can be prescribed for each, and if the aspirant follows the prescription he will be able to prove to himself the efficacy of the teachings. If you are an atheist, you are asked to believe in no credo, but to experiment with your mind. And whatever experience comes need not be named God; if you touch the bare fringes of infinity and become tranquil, call the experience X. If you are seeking a way to commune with your deity as a true Christian, Buddhist, or Hindu, then meditation is the test of your religion. If there is a God within, then she/he/it can be experienced. Meditation is the method that will open your mind to grace by pulling away the curtains of ego.

The question is often asked, why is it that at this time in the history of mankind the Eastern teachings are coming to the West? The question itself reveals an unawareness of the long tradition of Eastern teachers in the past several thousand years who have visited the leading civilizations of their time. For a brief history, please see Chapter One of our publication, *Meditation in Christianity.* Ancient Egypt, Iran, Greece, China, Rome, Russia, and Western Europe have all at the peak of their power received great yogis, and wondered at their unique way and perspective. These masters learned the languages of the dominant civilizations of their times and with an exceptional flexibility of mind and character blended their teachings with the culture and religion of the civilization they visited. It is in that very tradition that the masters of today visiting the dominant civilizations of our times are blending their teachings with and influencing the direction of science. There is no doubt that whatever civilization develops two thousand years from now will be given the teachings in whatever language man speaks and through the culture and manners he follows at that time.   In the experience of the meditative state, all language is silenced, and the true world religions are merely out-pourings from the minds that have touched infinity in meditation.

One of the greatest problems a seeker encounters today is to find a true teacher.   There is a dictum in the yoga tradition that one finds the teacher he deserves.   If one is not prepared to go through rigorous discipline and total self control of will, emotion, desire, and action, he will put the mantle of a teacher on someone who himself is not willing to undergo the strict disciplinary training and therefore advocates none.   Unfortunately, the word *guru* has become so commonplace in the English language that anyone who can touch his nose to his knees or who can pop a "nirvana pill" into his mouth is advertised as a guru.   This being the case, some of the greatest masters are trying to work in relative anonymity and accept only a select number of aspirants.   Their aim is not to herd the masses but to train and initiate a few chosen teachers.   However, there is such a proliferation of yoga classes and occult publications that it is hard for an average man on the street to find and recognize the genuine sources of the teachings.   Many of these teachers of yoga and the occult are in the same category as if a high school graduate from a village in India might take a three month freshman seminar in a U.S. college in the theory of nuclear physics, return to his homeland and train science teachers who in their turn may train others in the mysteries of nuclear science!

To avoid such pitfalls it is essential that an inquirer should go as close to the sources of the meditative teaching as possible. He should familiarize himself with the history of this tradition in its homeland and ask anyone claiming to be a teacher as to his own spiritual master, and his, and thus, back into antiquity. The second test should be to see for how long the teacher followed the disciplines under the master. Above all, third, is whether the teacher can initiate: which means, can he alter and induce states of higher consciousness in his disciples. Also, a true teacher of yoga will absolutely and uncompromisingly make it clear that psychedelic drugs are on the opposite end of the pole from meditation. In the former there is absolute loss of control over the mind, while the latter is absolute self-control of the mind. Through psychedelic drugs, one can hallucinate and injure his nervous system and brain. But with the help of meditation, one can strengthen the nervous system and co-ordinate the brain and make the mind one-pointed. The drug culture cannot help the student in experiencing the altered states of consciousness.

As stated above, the tradition of meditative teaching in a long, *unbroken* line of master/disciple relationships goes back many thousand years, and each monastery or school has maintained careful records of this lineage. For example, no one among the Brahmin priestly families of India can be married without being able to declare the name of the founder of the school of learning and sacred texts, forty centuries old, to which the prospective bride or bridegroom belongs. The same is true of the monastic lines. With each generation of masters, the knowledge has grown and it is imparted in sacred and code languages, the texts of which have not yet been translated. Even if these texts were translated by careful academic scholars, the true teaching would not come through because the scholars would not suspect that a certain code-word referred to a state of consciousness or to a mystic experience that cannot be conveyed to the non-initiate. The spiritual force and the tradition that gave birth to the rishis of the Vedas, to Zarathustra and the Buddha, continues at this time and will produce similar giants in the future. These adults of humanity do not arise out of a vacuum; they are the rare few stars who received such mighty initiations of the spiritual power at the hands of their own masters.

This tradition does not view the world and man as mere material shapes. Man's limbs are mere fan-blades whirling at the command of the energy flowing in a coil, the *kundalini*, or primal force. Here, think of a magnet on which you place a paper. Sprinkle some iron filings on this paper and they immediately arrange themselves in lines conforming to the magnetic force field. Each line in human personality is formed thus, along the force-field of the life-force, the consciousness-force. (It is for this reason that the Sanskrit texts on the science of personality take into account not only the form and figure but every minute line from head to toe; palmistry is a mere diluted Western version of this science.)

The meditative practice of the yogis are designed to heighten the intensity of this force-field which has 72,000 channels in man, of which the central-most, *sushumna*, flows through the spine. It is described as a pure white streak of lightning, 1/10,000th of a hair's breadth thick, from the base of the spine to the top of the head. As one receives a jolt from the highly intensified force-field of a master, the ego burns in the fire of knowledge, the mind is washed clean and then like Arjuna in the *Bhagavad-gita* (Chapters 9 - 11), the initiate experiences a cosmic vision and the light like millions of golden suns. Condense all that light into a pinhead in the center of a diamond and the master says to his disciple, "that luminous Self you are." *Tat tvam asi.* This initiation is referred to as *Shakti-Chalana*, quickening of the energies, and *Shakti-Pata*, descent of energies. This eternal line of initiations never started and shall never end. All the rest of the yoga teaching is of children playing with thimblesful of water on the shores of the cosmic ocean of divine energy.

The founding patriarch of this illumination of shaktis is no man, as the guru himself is not a person. The texts state categorically, "The *Golden Womb* alone is the teacher of yoga and no other." Whoever understands the meaning of the phrase, *"Golden Womb,"* he alone is a teacher of yoga. My own master, Venerable Swami Rama, is one of these founders of the yoga science, in whom the millenia of the history of the tradition of initiations continue to this day. Whatever mantras are given to the initiates today in any school of meditation are revelations received through the initiations into the *Golden Womb* of Mother Energy. And however many may pretend, only a few experience it. There is no method of meditation, no practice of yoga discipline, that is not included in this "royal path" or Raja Yoga. Each school claims the monopoly over the most effective method of meditational practice, but they all have originated from this one royal branch and return to it for a fresh infusion from century to century.

"Terrible is the face of the Lord, no one shall see it and yet live." Moses, too, was allowed a glimpse only of the Shadow of God. Arjuna pleaded to Krishna, "Desist; my surroundings are burning and I cannot endure this vision anymore. Please, divine Krishna, return to the gentle form that is familiar to me." The quickening of these cosmic energies is not for a man whose nerves have been weakened with uncontrolled passions and whose mind is a nest of the hornets of ego. If a piece of iron should wish to become a magnet, it must accept in total surrender the initiation of *Shakti-Pata*, the transfer of energy that the magnet would give it. Then the iron becomes a magnet, the disciple becomes a guru. How many are ready to take these steps? In our school of Superconscious Meditation we can only give a start to the seeker and hope that a few will have the courage to jump in and fewer yet the courage to cross the fiord.

This tradition of the masters has experimented in depth with the fullest realization of human potential, but the definition of human potential differs from that of the modern man. The man of today measures his power over his surroundings and wants to make steel pliable in his fingers and to explode uranium nuclei with a touch. To the yogi's mind, this may develop the fullest potential of steel and the nuclei, but his prime concern is to make man's body pliable, his breath prolonged, respiratory rhythms harmonious with cosmic rhythms, and to burst into the plane of divine energy by exploding with intense inner concentrations the foci of the barriers of mind.

II
Self and Personality

The ultimate aim of meditation is self-realization. It is, however, essential at this stage to define the term self-realization in order to clear a semantic problem that continues to persist between the teachers of meditation and the average Western student. The students use the word "self" to include the entire personality and especially to emphasize the physical personality. What do we mean when we say, "myself," "yourself"? In the Western mind, this means my body, nerves, brain, emotions, thoughts. When the body is sick, one says, "I am sick"; when the nerves are tense, one says, "I am nervous"; when the brain is agitated, we say, "I am disturbed." The idea of a self beyond and separate from these is intellectually, emotionally and spiritually difficult to grasp. It is for this reason that people go through a great many identity crises. The changes in one's environment, physical appearance, emotional feelings and intellectual thoughts seem to bring the idea of a change of identity. The identity is, then, dependent on a role that an individual is playing at a specific time and place in his relationships with others.

The meditational philosophy does not recognize any of these levels, experiences and reactions to be those of the self. So when the word "self-realization" is used, it conveys in the West the idea of realizing the fullest potential of human personality. What exactly is this human personality is a subject of speculation by great philosophers, but very few people in their daily lives go to the extent of defining personality—where does it begin, where does it end? These questions are seldom answered. The result is that, when students begin to meditate with the ultimate aim of self-realization, they are looking for results with which the teachers of the tradition have very little concern; even though some of these results may be by-products of the meditative practices, they are not meant to be the ultimate goals. Physical well-being, relaxation, improved concentration and memory—as well as other mental and so-called psychic powers—are all not what the masters are really after. It is for this reason that the tradition has defined the idea of self-realization with very great care, both in terms of analysis and spiritual experience, and there are vast volumes of philosophy in the Sanskrit language dedicated to the discussion of this question. If one does not fully understand the term self-realization, he will be totally confused as to the meaning of the term meditation.

Here we need to define "self" and "realization." However, there is a problem of the difference of opinion among the different schools of meditational philosophies which needs to be put in a proper perspective. Two of the major schools of the meditative philosophy are Vedanta and Sankhya.   In the Vedanta philosophy, the whole universe is a projection of the thought of one great, supreme Self known as Brahman whose own essential nature is threefold: existence, consciousness and bliss. All the differences attributed to the individual *jivas* or units of life-force among various living beings exist only temporarily on the level of an illusory reality and the transcendental experience is of the unity of all life-force. In the Sankhya system of philosophy, the material reality is entirely separate from the spiritual reality, and both these realities are coeval, coexistent and interacting. The multiplicity is real and not illusory.   In the Vedanta philosophy, ignorance and bondage consist of mistaking multiplicity where there is transcendental reality. In the Sankhya philosophy, the ignorance consists of the conscious individual self assuming a mistaken identity or identifying himself with the material nature.   In the Vedanta, the fullest enlightenment and liberation consist in realizing the supreme transcendental unity, whereas in the Sankhya it is the conscious individual self sorting out its true identity and discriminating between its self and the material nature, and recognizing that their apparent identity prior to the attainment of final discrimination was only an interaction.   In other words, the Sankhya recognizes the subject and the object to be completely separate, and spiritual ignorance consists of forgetting this separateness;   in the Vedanta, the separateness is illusory and must be transcended so that the subjective and the objective realities, the spiritual and the material existence are both emanations of the One

Supreme Self.   The question then arises as to which of these schools of philosophy should a meditator adhere to, and the answer is that both in the Sankhya and the Vedanta the first step consists of sorting out the subjective from the objective, discriminating between the Self and the non-Self.   Even though, in Vedanta, the transcendental reality is all Self, once the world comes into being, there is a dichotomy between the transcendental and the empirical, between the Absolute and the relative, between the conscious and the unconscious.   Once the individuation takes place, the individual spirit also must be recognized even if, in the ultimate realization, it will liberate itself from the bondage of such limitation.

Personality is not Self.   Personality is composite and an aggregate of many components.   The self is one, unalloyed.   The personality is material, the self is a spiritual energy.   The personality changes constantly, the self is unchanging.   The personality is transient, the self permanent.   The self is untouched, unaffected, ever pure, ever wise, ever free.   It is neither attracted nor averse to anything and is never in ignorance because its very nature is consciousness.   The personality is divided into many levels and planes, from the grossest to the finest, but the self is indivisible.   The *Bhagavad-gita* says that weapons cannot cleave it, fires cannot burn it, waters do not wet it, and winds do not dry it.   The personality is a garment, the self is the wearer.   The self's identification with the personality is ignorance and bondage.

Let us look at this false identification in the following diagram.

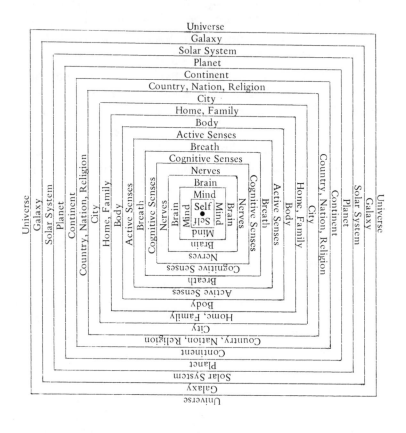

Why is it that you identify yourself with some of these squares more and with some a little less? Where in this universe do you begin and end? Where do you end and the rest of the world begin? It should be recognized that from the external-most limits of the universe to the mind it is all one material energy, that your relationship with the universe begins with the mind and, passing through the other instruments, it expands outwards. This extension is called action. What pours into the mind is called experience. The human personality consists of the seven innermost squares as above and relates to the rest of the squares. But this is not the true discrimination because we identify with many things in the outer squares also. Take, for example, the idea of being hurt. A person is hurt in the mind, in his feelings or in his body. A stone strikes the cranium, or a splinter gets into the toe and the person says, "I am hurt." Someone curses your favorite son and you also say, "I am hurt." Someone attacks your country and you say, "I am hurt." Someone challenges your religious beliefs and you say, "I am hurt." This shows that your identification is not limited to the seven innermost squares but includes many other squares depending on the circumstance. Why is it, then, that you include some of the squares in your personality and exclude some others? It would appear that in this type of thinking the definition of "I" is very flexible and ever-changing, but in the meditative philosophy none of these squares is the true "I." A man receiving a certain bank statement says, "I am rich" or "I am poor." Exactly where does this richness or poorness reside? If this "I" is only the first seven squares, he certainly does not deposit any money in his eyes or ears. Only when he extends his identification to something lying in the bank vault or in a safe can he think of himself as rich or poor. His richness and poverty now depend upon a few pieces of paper printed in a certain way at a certain place. A girl buys a beautiful new dress, puts it on and says, "I now look pretty." What looks pretty is the dress to which she, her own inner self, somehow extends the beauty, life and light of the innermost self. This association alone can be the explanation for all the jewelry and cosmetics that are employed to prop up our idea of beauty.

We see in this way that we identify with many things that are external to us and through this process of identification we internalize them. It is, of course, not possible for us to internalize the money bills or the dress in a physical sense—we cannot store them inside our bodies or inside our craniums—the internalization is in the mind. The question then arises, is it not possible that some other things also, which we consider as permanent parts of our personality, are merely fixtures like the furnishings of a house, the dress on a body, or money in a bank vault? Is it possible that our relationship to our skin, blood, bones, eyes, ears and the grey matter called brain may be the same as our relationship with the furnishings, dresses and money and that these, too, are alterable states of relationships, mere assumptions of identity about which there is nothing permanent, nothing forever true? According to the meditative philosophy, this, indeed, is the case. This identity of the personality is just as flexible and changing as the state of richness or poverty, prettiness or ugliness depending on the color of dress.   What is the difference between body and non-body, something that is my body and that is not my body? What is the difference between becoming pretty by wearing a dress, putting on cosmetics or changing the hair style?   Let us take this progressively, gradually, closer and closer to our physical personality.

The dress and the cosmetics are definitely things external to the personality but somehow we manage to attach them to ourselves and identify our appearances with them and them with our appearances. But now we come even closer to the body. A woman is hurt because her lover did not notice her new hair style. She identifies herself with her hair so she beautifies it and has it done one way or another by a stylist. She pays a great deal of attention to it, where it curls, how if flows, how long it hangs on her shoulders or on her back and spends a great deal of time beautifying herself by changing her hair style. Is that hair truly a part of her personality? What happens when she cuts off a portion of her hair? Does she still identify with it? Does she keep that cut-off portion and brush it daily as part of her self-beautification? We see here clearly a case of mistaken identity. As long as something is attached to the body it is part of the personality, and as soon as it is detached, cut off, removed, it ceases to be part of the personality even though the hair has no sensation or feeling whether it is hanging on the shoulder or cut off and thrown away.

The rest of our limbs cannot thus be cut off except

when they have to be amputated, but does the personality of a man whose leg has been amputated change? Does he become somebody else? As long as he identifies himself with whatever his idea of his personality is, he remains that person.

Like the hair, our body cells are also undergoing constant change. Uncounted numbers of our cells die out each day, and new cells are created. No one at the age of 20 has the same cells that he had at the age of 2. No one at the age of 60 has the same cells he had at the age of 20. Like the bank book, the dresses, the hair cut off or the leg amputated, the body cells, too, have been changing so it cannot be said that I have the same legs or the same spine that I had twenty years ago. Then who is it that continues to say, "I"? What is there to prove that this "I" is the same person who played with his brother or sister as a child, or who married a young man or woman in youth and now lies on a bed dying, for have we not died each time our body cells have undergone a complete turnover? In meditative philosophy, one takes these questions with a great deal of seriousness in order to identify the innermost "I."

It is obvious that none of these various elements of personality conforms to the definition of Self given in the meditative systems of philosophy. None of these aspects of personality is ever-pure, ever-wise, ever-free; they are attached, averse to, affected, subject to change. In none of them an absolute and perfect consciousness can be detected. They are subject to the vagaries of relativity. There is absolutely no transcendental reason why they should come into being and cease to be. Though the scientist may answer the question of how they come into being, he is at a loss as to why, for what ultimate end? The ultimate end of the personality, *purusha*, is the innermost spiritual being, the Self.

The meditative process, however, is not a denial of personality but the fullest possible development and unfoldment of this personality, the total illumination of all the powers latent in the personality. Here, take for illustration a candle around which a set of curtains is hanging and, again, another set of curtains, and another, and yet another. Though the candle has the power to illuminate the entire room, the curtains are the obstructions between the walls and the light. As the curtains are removed one by one, the light spreads and illuminates larger and larger areas, and when the final curtain is removed, the walls also are illuminated. Assuming that each square represents a set of curtains, meditation is a process of removing these curtains so that the light of the self may spread. In other words, the development of personality does not take place by dependence on the surroundings and the environment nor on what is fed into the mind from these external surroundings. It depends, rather, on how well the personality, which is external to self, can receive the light from that candle of self which is the center. But if light forgets its own self-luminosity and identifies with the curtains, then the light visible outside those curtains will be of the color of the curtains. Without removing the curtains, the true color of light cannot be ascertained intellectually or experienced spiritually. This experience of the purest nature of light is called discrimination, enlightenment, and liberation.

This discrimination does not come overnight, and in order to reach this point one must work on the gradual purification of personality. It means freeing the consciousness from false identification, both with the material universe around and the unconscious part of one's own personal being. What do we mean by the unconscious part of personal being? The personality, by itself without the self, is all unconscious. The mind, too, is not regarded as a conscious force but the finest modification of matter. So a yogi does not speak of mind over matter, but spirit over matter including the mind. A yogi also does not speak of cosmic consciousness because cosmos is also matter, empirical reality, external. He speaks of realizing the transcendental level of the cosmic appearance. Meditation is a process whereby the mind also realizes that any appearance of consciousness in it is on loan from the self. It is because of the self that the mind becomes active which, in turn, activates the brain cells and the nervous system and loans out a little of life and consciousness to the rest of the body. When the self withdraws its rays, like a turtle withdrawing its limbs, the body becomes unconscious. The reason that many physical processes are suspended in the highest states of meditation is because the self withdraws its power leaving to the personality just enough energy to survive while the self becomes even more deeply aware of itself.

The physical personality is extremely limiting for the self. As the self withdraws to the awareness of self-luminosity, its consciousness is, then, not "expanded," it comes to know its fullest extent and recognizes itself to be the source of all life and consciousness that previously seemed to belong to the personality.

III
Purification
of Personality

We have said above that meditation is a process of purifying the personality. Purifying it of what? There is a word in the yoga philosophy, *klesha*. This word means both a stain and a pain. We are all aware of the suffering that each individual undergoes. On this point, both the Buddhists and the followers of the Sankhya and Vedanta philosophies agree—that a master of meditation is moved to helping others out of deep compassion because he has freed himself of the entire process of sorrow and pain and cannot help but work consistently to remove the pain of others. He regards ignorance to be the true cause of all pain. A personality that is *klishta*, in pain, is a personality that has stains, lacking in the fullest realization of the pure nature of the innermost self.

We cannot discuss personality without understanding the essential nature of mind. In the West, one often hears of mind over matter. The yogis, instead, speak of spirit or consciousness over matter, which includes mind. Mind is the finest vibration of material energy. It is the messenger of heaven to earth and of earth to heaven. It brings the subtlety of the spirit to the grossness of the body and the grossness of the body close to the spirit. It bridges the within and the without, speaking the language of both countries. Mind is a mirror in which the spirit sees its own face. When the mind gathers an impression of the blue, it turns, as it were, blue; and the spirit, seeing the reflection, mistakes itself to be blue. The mind gathers the impression of red and the spirit sees that it is red. By understanding mind and its functions, one will understand all one's problems, aspirations, and seeking. When the mind has ceased to gather impressions, it turns away from the world to the spirit within and there is no more wishing, only a will, a free will.

The aim of yoga is freedom, liberation, salvation, but once again, we are engaged in a semantic problem: the yogi advises absolute freedom and people think it means, "Do whatever you want to do." In fact the freedom of will means *not* to be subject to your wantings and the vagaries of wishes. Often when one says, "This is my choice, my free choice," he does not know that his will is in fact bound to a false identity and a false layer of personality. It is like water in a blue bottle saying, "It is my choice to appear blue." Likewise, you 'freely' believe in some things because you have gathered the raw material in your personality for that conclusion, and you will draw no other conclusion. One person goes through an experience and draws one conclusion, and another person draws a different conclusion from the same experience. The experience is like litmus paper that turns blue in alkaline solutions and pink in the acidic, not by its own free choice, but because of the agents which were brought into its proximity. A certain prejudice in favor of, or against, a conclusion is ready-built in the sum total of your personality. We are bound, the will is bound, to what we have gathered into ourselves as the residue of actions and experiences. What we have taken into our personality, only that we project outwards. Whatever personality one has, the way he moves, sits or talks is an expression of the sum total of the residue of all his actions and experiences of a lifetime and, if you believe in reincarnation, of many lifetimes.

A master, a liberated one, has no personality, and this is so overpowering that all personalities bow humbly in his presence and court his favor. Such power would be dangerous in the hands of the unliberated, for if the master wants to excite them, they become excited, and if he wants to pacify them, they become pacified. You say, "Oh, what an attractive personality!" and yet the one thing this personage does not consist of is the shell of personality. Because he does not act from the subconscious, his superconscious flows directly into his conscious, without intervening layers of the darkness of the subconscious. A Christ has no subconscious, therefore no dark little corners and niches full of cobwebs and dirt. He is transparent so that the superconscious flows through his conscious unhindered and its light is visible and clear, its joy is catching and infectious. That is a Master, the man of freedom, *mukta*, without bondage. He also controls all matter, including the mind.

The raw material of thought is twofold: reflection and reaction. All experience is a reflection. In Sanskrit it is called *raga*: attraction, attachment, a process of coloring. The word *raga* comes from the Sanskrit verb root *ranj*, cognate to the English verb *to long*. The word *raga* also means color, so it is a word for coloring, for longing, for reflecting, for attractions and attachments. When you love someone, what happens? His or her color reflects in the mirror of your mind. The spirit sees that color in the mind and says, "I am in love." It is much as a lake appears blue or pink as the colors of the rays reflect in it. Although the lake itself is actually colorless, for the time being you forget that the water is transparent and without color. The personality means a colored mind. A pure mind is a clear mind, so all the intuition and godly knowledge can flow through it. A colored mind is a befogged mind. It is colored with everything you see, hear, touch, taste, smell, or otherwise experience. The residue of all those colors has painted the surface of the mind. What kind of a painting is it? Take a clean and clear glass and throw on it a splash of yellow, of red, and blue, and again of yellow, pink or purple, and green. Such has become your personality over a lifetime of gathering experiences indiscriminately from the morning of childhood to the autumn of old age. Throughout life the only thing we do is paint our minds with such indiscriminate colors. As you read this, what is happening? The colors splashing on the mind are becoming part of the personality, creating the personality. This is called reflection, reflecting of colors on the mind, *raga*, attachment, attraction.

In yoga philosophy, all nature, external or personal

and mental, has three fundamental attributes. Creation is a compounding of these in varying proportions to produce different objects and mental personalities. For details of these, see the *Bhagavad-gita*, chapters 14, 17 and 18. But here, briefly, the three attributes, called *gunas*, are:

sattva	harmony, purity, light, symbolized in white or crystal;
rajas	activity, active energy, movement, agitation, symbolized in red;
tamas	darkness, dullness, stagnation, inertia, stability, symbolized in deep blue or black.

A mental personality may thus be *sattvic, rajasic* or *tamasic*, depending on what coloring of impressions it has received.

Here the reader is asked to participate in a brief experiment.

Think in your mind of some event which was very pleasant, calming, peaceful and harmonious. Think of this for, say, 30 seconds, and it will bring you to a normal, natural, quietude of mind and a smile to your lips. This *sattvic* thought will produce a *sattvic* mood.

Now change the thought, and think in your mind again for 30 seconds of some very exciting memory of an event of agitation that had made you jump and shout "hurray." This *rajasic* thought will produce a *rajasic* mood.

Think again for 30 seconds and bring forth the memory of some dark, dull, slothful moment. This *tamasic* thought will produce a *tamasic* mood.

Thus you have added 30 seconds each of *sattvic* white, *rajasic* red and *tamasic* blue to your personality.

The other part of the raw material of thought is reaction. There may be many people sitting in a room having many things in common, yet their reactions to the same experience differ. Two readers are not reading the same message in these sentences.

The reflection of a blue object in a yellow mirror is neither blue nor yellow, and the color of the reflection is no indication of either the color of the mirror or of the object. Utter the word God in a company of friends and someone thinks, are we still in the Middle Ages? But in another person, some chord in the heart is struck and echos reverently "God." It is like litmus paper changing colors in acid or in alkaline solution, even though the litmus paper is the same.

There are twenty persons in a room. Someone walks in the door; nothing happens to nineteen. But he is one person's husband or close friend or enemy. The reaction is entirely different. Watch your reaction and you learn to guide your emotional thoughts. It is not the content of the mental personality of that person alone which causes your reactions, but the colors of your mind which produce a color that is originally neither entirely your own nor entirely of the object or of the person being experienced. For an average human being, it is very difficult to define where reflection or experience ends and where a reaction begins. The two are interwoven. The boundary lines between the two are very slim. At what point do you complete absorbing the sight of a rose and begin to react to its color?

Your reactions also invite certain experiences to which you react again. This vicious cycle between reflection and reaction is seldom broken. And in this manner, your personality is being created every moment of your life. Its little daily modulations are unnoticeable, but as you gather the raw material of personality and thought over a period of years, the sum total shows at the end of the period. How does one break this vicious cycle? By making a careful choice of one's experiences; that is, selecting what colors from the world of objects and persons you want to reflect in your mind and then observing and gradually directing your reactions. One must make a decision as to what type of personality he wishes to cultivate. If you want to make of yourself a lovable personality, then choose the reflections and reactions accordingly. While reading this, you may make a decision: from now on, I wish to add, as it were, such and such 'chemicals' to my personality; I shall read this kind of book; keep a certain kind of company; wear only a particular type of perfume or burn a certain scent of incense; that I shall speak only such words with such tone modulation; that I shall listen to such music; and that I shall avoid that other kind of exciting attitude, destructive words, sounds, thoughts, and combinations; that I shall look with greater attention and concentration at certain types of objects and avoid looking at certain other types of objects. Gradually, these experiences will be added to the sum total of the personality and the thoughts arising in the mind will have a different total content.

What we have described above is, of course, discipline. It is practiced not only by cloistered nuns, celibates in the ashrams, or sages in the hermitages. You may make your choice anywhere at any time, and do it not as an enforced discipline, but as a choice of experiences and reactions conducive to cultivating the type of personality you most desire. As these changes occur in your personality, they show on your face, in your choice of the color of your tie or the shade of your curtains, in your movement, gait, and modulated voice. These again become the magnetic currents that draw their complement to you and attract towards you what you desire to gather around your personality. What you gather is again added to the sum total of your person. In this way, the entire amalgam of your personality, which is formed of the residue of all your actions and experiences, reflections and reactions, changes its composition and gradually an undisturbed and saintly personality is formed. The hundred causes for sorrow and the thousand causes for joy that one saw each day in his life no longer appear to be so appetizing. The entire process of reaction is now different. For example, normally one runs away from the wolf, that is the reaction of the untrained mind. But Saint Francis did not have to *force* himself to go and pat the wolf on the head and address him as Brother Wolf. It was no discipline for him. The entire content of his mind was such that his natural reaction was that of love for the normally violent creature. He was, in fact, not reacting; he was not acting out of the motivations of a pre-conditioned mind. And to his self-dependent action arising from within the center of the self, the wolf's reaction was naturally non-violent. One normally does not want to lift a scorpion with his hand. But there is a parable in India of a saint who, bathing in the river, saw a scorpion in the water struggling to come out. Because of natural compassion, he was moved to lift the scorpion in his hand but the scorpion stung him, the hand shook and the scorpion fell back into the water to continue its struggles. The saint was again moved by compassion, lifted the scorpion and was stung again. Someone ashore asked why the saint persisted in torturing himself, and the answer was: "If the scorpion cannot change his nature, why should I?" This type of altered reaction is not in fact reaction at all, but action from within the deeper self. All the rules of moral discipline imposed upon a disciple are part of the training to cultivate such a mind.

There is another example of pure reaction to an impure situation. When the Buddha was training his monks to go out and teach to the world, at one point in their training, he asked: "If you go to a city where people do not wish to attend your preaching and completely ignore you, what will you do?" Their answer was: "We shall consider them very compassionate people for they are giving us the opportunity to enjoy our solitude." The Buddha asked: "What if they did not give alms and your begging bowls remained empty?" And they said: "We shall thank them for allowing us to undertake a fast." Again the Buddha asked: "Suppose they throw stones at you?" They replied: "We shall bless them for their kindness in not killing us outright." "And," asked the Buddha, "if they indeed rush to kill you?" The monks' final reply was: "We shall regard it as a deed of kindness for they are liberating us from a useless body that in any case is not eternal, nor a source of wisdom." This type of non-violent reaction would require much greater courage if it were not a natural reaction, if it were forced. But for a carefully cultivated, saintly personality this is the only mode of behavior. Not because of a court.

Discipline, then, is excluding certain 'chemicals' and adding certain other 'chemicals' to your personality which are conducive to its purification.

Is this discipline adding color or washing color off? The answer is in the word *vairagya*, dispassion, the antonym of *raga* or color. *Vairagya* is defined in the Yoga Sutras of Patanjali as a control over the reflections and reactions established by a masterful spirit where the mind no longer turns in craving to:

the objects one experiences or has heard of. The objects one experiences are of form, taste, smell, sound or touch (property, power, sex, and so forth). The objects one has heard of may be of two kinds: 1) Not to be experienced with the current body; such as heaven or the spirit's enjoyment of the undifferentiated, unmanifest matter-energy field. 2) Those experienced with the current body but in a different state of awareness; such as celestial sounds, celestial fragrances, and so forth.

There are four stages of *vairagya* or dispassion:

Yatamana (effort): The mental disposition such as attraction or aversion dwelling in the *citta*, in the mind's pool, induce the senses to turn towards the external objects even when the objects are not present. In the first stage of dispassion, one counters these mental dispositions reinforcing the idea of their undesirability, their being causes of pain and defilement, and repeatedly introduces the positive counter-thoughts, thus slowly preventing the mind from inducing the senses to turn to the external objects.

Vyatireka (self analysis): The seeker analyzes and learns to recognize:
a) so many of the defilements and pains have now been cleansed off,
b) such and such are now in the process of being washed off, and
c) these certain ones, however, are yet to be worked on.
Ekendriya (dormant): The painful defilements and dispositions are no longer strong enough to turn the senses towards their objects but remain dormant and potentially explosive, awaiting a time when the senses may again be in the proximity of the objects, so that they may be turned towards them. The senses turn towards the objects only when the objects are present.
Vashikara (mastery): When the attractions and aversions are completely turned off to the extent that not only the material but also the celestial objects are no longer found to be attractive, and even when they are present, the yogi is totally indifferent towards them. That stage is called the Mastery. Then the self says, "They are objects of my control and not I ever under their control."

Vairagya is a prerequisite for any great progress on

the path of meditation and spiritual development. However, the human mind is not capable of washing off all its colors in the initial stages of the practice. Therefore, one learns to make the choice of the kind of colors to be added, rather than totally eliminating them in the beginning. The *tamas* is transcended by *rajas*, the *rajas* by *sattva* and as the personality becomes more and more *sattvic*, it is progressively refined and purified and the meditation becomes easier. The *tamas* that was at first the cause of dullness and stagnation now becomes a stabilizer of *sattva*. *Rajas* that was first agitating now helps the progress forward and the pure self begins to reflect in the crystal of *sattva*. Then no further colors are added. The state of *apara vairagya*, supreme dispassion, is reached. When the highest *samadhi* is reached, the supreme dispassion is experienced in this way: I have found all there is to be found; all pains and defilements have disappeared; segment by segment, I have completely cut the possibility of the continuation of transitions in the endless cycle of worldly existence. No further disciplines are necessary. Then renunciation too is renounced. As a Persian poet has said, "Cut out cravings; cut out the experiences; cut out all logic; cut out all teaching; cut out the discipline; and then cut the cutting out." This is the final liberation, but until we reach that point, we must continue to refine and purify the personality to make it a fit vehicle of the altered state of consciousness leading to self-realization.

Thus, the four noble truths of the Buddha are equally recognized in the philosophy of the Yoga Sutras

of Patanjali.   A yogi is motivated by the need to remove
the pain of all beings, realizing the four-fold truth of pain,
cause of pain, removal and means of removing the pain.
Vyasa, the ancient commentator on the Yoga Sutras, says
that just as medical science has four aspects: disease,
cause of disease, removal of disease and means of removing disease, so the science of liberation (*Moksha-
shastra*) also has these four aspects regarding pain.   The
psychological system of the meditative philosophy begins
and ends with this.   All painful thoughts are symptomatic
of the stains of ignorance in the personality.   If a person
on the path of meditation wants to know how pure or
impure his personality is, he should watch carefully how
many painful thoughts arise in his mind.   It is not the
material or physical suffering which is a yogi's first pre-
occupation because he believes that the material and
physical suffering is only an extension of the state of
human thought, individually or collectively.   It is in the
thoughts that the suffering must first be removed, and it
cannot be removed unless the stains on the instruments
of the processes of thinking and experiencing within the
personality are washed off.   All pain, produced from the
environment and brought into the personality or projected
from the personality into the environment is a result only
of these impure states of personality.   If there is a pain,
there is a stain.   Wash the stain, there is no more pain.
These pain-causing stains, the *kleshas*, are fivefold:

> *Avidya*: Ignorance
> > Mistaking the eternal for non-eternal,
> > non-eternal for eternal

	Mistaking pure for impure, impure for pure

             Mistaking pure for impure, impure for pure
             Mistaking pleasure for pain, pain for pleasure, and
             Mistaking self for non-self, non-self for self.

Asmita: False I-ness
             As if the consciousness force, the self, and the object of consciousness such as personality and the world are one.

Raga: Attachment
             Brooding on the pleasures which are wrongly defined as under Ignorance above.

Dvesha: Aversion
             Brooding on pains, also wrongly defined under the influence of Ignorance.

Abhinivesha: Fear of death
             May I not cease to be: this fear because of the memory of the death of the last incarnation.

All other fears, insecurities, emotional disturbances, agitations, and complexes arise out of the above five. All attachments for physical sensations, derived from the environment and the surroundings through the doors of the senses and all aversions to the feelings and sensations similarly derived create many psychological problems. As one travels on the path of purification, one washes the stains of wrong identification and ignorance and thereby is less and less affected by this fivefold aggregate of *klesha*.

This purification in itself may be somewhat of a painful process, at least initially, until one begins to enjoy the light that comes from within. Disciplines of the body, rules of restraint, curbing of emotional turmoils, practices of sublimation and mindfulness, a code of moral behavior, a regular practice of meditation are some of the processes of this purification. As the light of the self begins to penetrate through these layers of personality, the personality undergoes certain processes of purification described below without too much effort and struggle. These processes are the increased sensitivity of the senses, and control of that sensitivity is achieved. More of the light of self comes down to the senses, yet the self no longer says, "I am the senses," but rather, "I control the senses and give them their light and their life." Unfortunately, we live in a world where people have forgotten the meaning of *rasa*, the true essence, the spiritual juice of the orange that is the material universe. What kind of crazy country will that be where people extract the juice of an orange, throw the juice away and eat the husk exclaiming about the taste of that husk, not realizing they have thrown away the juice because of which a little of that taste remains in the husk? We, too, forget that the essence of all pleasure is the joy of the supreme consciousness and, in enjoying the senses, we are only tasting the husk in which only a fraction of the *rasa* and *ananda*, the joyful juice of divinity, remains.

It is believed in the meditative tradition that the only pleasure in the world consists of concentration. If you do not believe this, you may try an experiment. Eat your food without concentrating on the taste buds and then eat also with concentration on the taste buds, and you will know what the true pleasure consists of. Smell a flower absent-mindedly and then smell it with concentration. Look at a painting with eyes roving at random and then look at its beauty with the fullest concentration on specific parts in a certain order even though this type of concentration requires discipline. The pleasure of sex, too, is nothing but that of concentration, and the moment of greatest pleasure, that of an orgasm, consists of total concentration of the partner on the feelings. Where there is no love, there is no concentration and then no pleasure in the mere physical movement of sex.

As the self frees itself of false identification with the physical body, it is less and less affected by the sloth or sickness because it is able to command the states of the body. Many people dream of commanding the states of consciousness before they have begun to command the states of the body, and yet a mind in an undisciplined body is very difficult to discipline. There are certain definite changes that take place in the physical habits of a meditative person. Some of these are: a regular and deep breath, regular bowel movement, a regular habit of eating and drinking in moderation with much less dependence on material energy produced by food or an emotional fulfillment through food, less sleep and almost no physical laziness or sloth. Such a person sits and walks erect and the muscles of his body are completely relaxed. A person whose forehead shows wrinkles of worry, who gesticulates a great deal, moves his fingers unnecessarily and fiddles about is not a man of meditation. A meditative person is totally aware of everything that his body is doing.

The next step is the control of the conscious mind. The habits of the conscious mind feed the subconscious thus forming our external personalities, and then that subconscious in turn overcomes the conscious mind. Thus, a meditative person is extremely careful of what he feeds into his mind through the senses of perception. He selects his field of experiences and only those things that will aid in the process of his purification, removal of false identification, liberating him from dependence on the environment that he perceives, are made welcome into his mind. Thus he is conscious of what he studies, sees, hears, touches and in what way he cultivates his reactions to these perceptions. At this point, he trains himself carefully to recognize all the guises in which his six enemies present themselves: passion, anger, greed, delusion and attachment, pride and malice. In the system of meditational psychology, these are the six painful thoughts or emotions in man, and wherever these are present, as stated below, there exist stains on the sheet of the mind.

The first step in washing the mind is to recognize the presence of these stains in oneself. Unfortunately, each one of us has the habit of first denying and then justifying their presence. The steps in this process of purification are as follows:

      1)   Ceasing to deny their presence

      2)   Ceasing to justify their presence

3)   Not feeling guilty about their presence but working on purification.

Recognizing one's imperfections is like recognizing the faults in a motor vehicle one is driving. As soon as one becomes aware of faulty steering or faulty brakes, he takes steps to make the repairs so that he may reach his destination. Similarly, as soon as one becomes aware of one's painful thoughts, he recognizes that they arise because of conflicts of duality and the dichotomies that he himself has created. Through meditation, he learns to depend less and less on the external environment. As the *Lawbook of Manu* says, the only definition of pain and pleasure is that dependence is pain and non-dependence is pleasure. When one depends on things of his surroundings for establishing his identity, this dependence causes painful reactions in the mind because the self is not dependent on anything else for its light and continuously seeks to overcome the dependence of the physical personality on the material environment. This is what creates the dichotomy. Through meditation, one realizes: my worth is not in my professional accomplishments, hairstyling, color of dress or the number of money bills deposited in my name at the bank. It is not even in my name, because the names are also transitory, mere assumptions of the parents accepted by the rest of society. Poor or rich, tall or short, handsome or ugly, successful or a failure in the chosen profession, these are mere conditions of the external personality and not of the self. As one begins to look at the external squares from the progressively inward squares rather than the other way 'round as is the common habit, the personality becomes naturally purified, and through increased sensitivity one becomes more and more aware of the faults in the vehicle of his personality which he must perfect in order to reach his spiritual goal.

In other words, meditation cannot be divorced from life and life cannot be separated from meditation. Many people hope to increase the depth of their meditation without purifying those aspects of their personalities which interact with their external lives, and when they do not succeed in meditation, they often give up the entire idea of such a spiritual practice. It must be remembered that in the process of exploration of personality the meditator cannot help but encounter all the hidden thoughts and complexes which come to the surface, and the purpose of this encounter is to draw the aspirant's attention to the stains which need to be washed and cleansed off.

If one wants to know at what stage of spiritual development he really is, he should first learn to recognize which of the five stages of the activity of his mind he experiences on the average in his normal life as well as in meditation. These five stages are:

Delusion and dullness, *mudham*
Distracted, random thoughts, *kshiptam*
Thought in the process of purification, *vikshiptam*
One-pointed concentration, *ekagram*
Cessation of the waves of the mind, *niruddham*

The chart on pages 50 and 51 will further define these terms and explain the attendant signs and symptoms of the sickness or health of the mind.

For a spiritual master the aim of meditation, then, is not just the increased sensitivity of the senses or an emotional balance or the powers such as extrasensory perception. The person who has embarked on a spiritual path has only one goal—to know the purity of self and to discriminate between the self, which is spiritual energy, and non-self including the mental and physical personality which are modifications of matter.

Some more questions need to be answered here. First, what about the Buddhist doctrine of non-self? From the point of view of Superconscious Meditation the question can concern only someone who has already advanced to the point where he has transcended his external personality. We might say that, through the Buddhist doctrine of *anatta*, non-self, one will recognize that what he thought of as self, the composite personality consisting of form, sensations, feeling, impressions and awareness, not only decomposes, but that these components are not the self. It will take a long period of practice even to rise above this imposition of self on non-self. When one has reached that point and the material and mental personality has been transcended, only then can one determine through his own experience where any other permanent conscious self exists beyond or does not. If there is such a conscious self according to one's own spiritual experience, then also one can determine through experience again whether it reincarnates or not. As one proceeds to explore the self-luminescent light of this self, one also finds out whether it is an individual self each separate in the various personalities or whether

THE FIVE STAGES OF THE NATURAL EVOLUTION OF CHITTA,

Name	Predominant guṇa	Stage	Samādhi or non-samādhi	Type of vṛttis
Mūḍham (overcome with delusion)	Tamas (rajas and sattva secondary)	Sleep, fear, slothfulness, depression, delusion	(Vyutthāna) random life non-samādhi	Sarvārtha (random thoughts, objects)
Kṣhiptam (distracted random thought)	Rajas (tamas and sattva secondary)	Grief, flightiness, inability to concentrate; worry; sorrow; involvement with small affairs of the world.	non-samādhi	Sarvārtha
Vikṣhiptam (process of purification)	Sattva (tamas and rajas secondary)	Joy, clarity, forgiveness, deep faith, steadfastness, strength, absence of depression, generosity, alertness.	Still non-samādhi but the beginnings of samādhi (a transitional state.)	Still Sarvārtha, but beginnings of one-pointedness.
Ekāgram (one-pointed concentration)	Sattva (rajas and tamas subdued and reduced to mere potential)	Neutrality, equanimity, neither joy nor sorrow.	Samprajnāta samādhi (samādhi with seed)	One-pointedness
Niruddham (cessation of vṛttis)	No more transmutations of guṇas.	See *Yoga Sutras*, Ch. 1 Sutra 3 (self realizes self)	Asamprajnāta samādhi (seedless samādhi)	Cessation of all vṛttis, therefore, no object and no one-pointedness

ACTIVITIES, HABITS, DISPOSITIONS OF DAILY LIFE

Natural or unnatural to chitta	Type of people	Ethics	Disposition
Unnatural	Base, low people	Based on four things: Kama (passion) Krodha (anger) Lobha (greed) Moha (delusion)	Ignorance anaishvarya (non-godliness); ajnāna (not based on precepts of knowledge); adharma (not based on laws); raga (attachment)
Unnatural	Normal, average people	Attraction and Aversion	Halfway between knowledge and ignorance (transition state); conflict
Unnatural	More evolved people (seekers)	Non-attachment, desireless actions	Jnāna (knowledge) dharma (law) vairagya (beginnings of dispassion) aisvarya (godliness, no conflict)
Natural	Yogis	Aparavairāgya (lower dispassion)	Correct knowledge of the true nature of things.
Neither natural nor unnatural, chitta in its own form.	Higher Yogis	Paravairāgya (supreme, final dispassion)	No disposition See. Ch. 1, Sutra 3

the individual units of the life force are sparks and waves in the one, single infinite, immanent in the empirical cosmic experience and in the transcendental reality.

The first step in all schools of meditation is the purification of personality, and the final goal is to recognize, not through intellectual approaches but in a spiritual experience the true nature of the reality of consciousness. In English, one says, "I have a soul." In the Yoga tradition, "I have a body; I am the soul." If you say, "I have a soul," who is it who has the soul? Who is speaking? I am the self. I have the body and the personality. In the past, I have falsely thought of things happening to the body and the personality as happening to the self, but now let me go inwards and look.

IV
System of
Superconscious
Meditation

The methods of Superconscious Meditation, based on the tradition of Raja Yoga, are taught in all their aspects in a system divided into various steps. These are explained below.

Emotional Balance: Yamas and Niyamas

A harmonious personality is always emotionally balanced. Conflicts of duality and dichotomies are the source, sign and result of neurosis. It is true that there have been only a few figures in history who have been totally free of conflict: Krishna, Christ, Buddha and a few other masters, but one must start wherever he is. In the training of yoga, an emotionally balanced personality is developed through the application of a number of disciplines and meditative practices. In an ashram situation, where disciples live under guidance, a number of methods are employed by the teachers to reduce the involvement with emotional conflict. Here it is not a matter of making a choice and reviewing a commitment every day. The disciple has already made the choice of becoming a disciple and has come seeking a discipline.

Discipline

Service

Practice

are the three pillars of the spiritual palace one builds for oneself when living in an ashram. Of these, discipline may include such aspects as a strict daily schedule, total control over desires and passions, obedience to the teacher, total non-involvement with acts, experiences and relationships that are not conducive to spiritual progress. The meetings with outsiders are permitted only rarely and equanimity in all situations is the first prerequisite of a continued stay.

Service means to surrender one's time and energies to whatever is needed to be done. One does not live as a guest but as a careful host, aware of everything that needs to be done. Yet, through all the burdens of running a home, one must find time to complete the spiritual practice prescribed by the guru. Idling is not resting but rusting, and the only type of sleep permitted in an ashram is either (i) the sleep of total exhaustion after a day of discipline, service and practice; or (ii) the yoga sleep.

It may be argued that one learns more from life than from total seclusion. The teachers are certainly aware of this. The training in an ashram prepares one for going out into life in such a way that meaningless relationships and the necessary but difficult actions, and random experiences do not distract one from the chosen path; they teach one the right and positive lessons rather than merely eliciting a mixed and confusing reaction. Those disciples who are not fortunate enough to live under the direct guidance available in an ashram learn through life. As with an ashramite, so also with this second category of disciples who must live a life of action in the world, it is always true that one is placed by the guru into a life situation where she or he must come face to face with all that lies latent within the subconscious and what flows from the superconscious. The conflicts must be resolved through the application of certain moral principles.

There are several ways in which these methods of developing a person differ from modern psychotherapy. One, the test of a right choice is not "what is pleasant to me," but what is right and beneficial for *all* involved in a situation. A person is taught that the transitory nature of the "pleasant" in life precludes it from being a valid test for eternal values. Two, the practice of meditation itself has the effect of bringing a resolution of personality. This is not the resolution of a specific problem. The philosophy of meditation is not issue-oriented. It changes the personality and thereby brings about the natural change in perspective. A specific problem may remain as it was around us, but the person responds to it differently.

The effects take place on many levels: (i) physiological changes are caused through the practices of physical discipline, breathing, relaxations and meditation so that the muscles, nerves and brain are naturally more relaxed. It has been found that tension-producing and tension-produced chemicals are found in much less strength in the blood of meditative people. (ii) Philosophical change includes a change in the values of life so that one's endless pursuit of external things and desires which previously led to equally endless frustrations just ceases. The only aim in life thereafter is the realization of Self, and helping others to free themselves from pains by giving them similar resolution of personality. Then one's prayer is, "I seek not a kingdom, nor paradise, nor freedom from the chain of re-incarnations; I pray only that the suffering of all the beings of the world ceases." (iii) The psychological change is the resolution of personality as described above. It cannot be separated from the physiological changes. In fact, a person with a sound philosophy of life can never be psychologically confused because his actions are guided from an inner principle. A teacher of meditation does not explore the history of each complex a person suffers from. He does not count each wrinkle but smoothes the entire fabric of the mind to change the mode of the entirety of its activity. How that is accomplished is seen only when the actual techniques of meditation are taught. (iv) The religious change cannot be ignored here. The commitment to a personal philosophy of life is prevented from becoming a fanaticism and an evangelism because one looks for eternal values of the meditative experience from which all religion has begun. One is not converted to a religion, nor giving up one's own religious mode, but rather is finding within one's own experience the God within—proof for the validity of truths stated by all great sages and mystics of all lands and of all the centuries. Meditation is the only test and the only proof of the existence of an Eternal Principle within. (v) The moral change is just another mode of psychological change. Very few people today realize that they have reached a viewpoint concerning the definition of a moral life not on the basis of a rational approach but as an emotional reaction, as a result of their own psychological problems. As the psychological personality is resolved, the need to escape from self-discipline is no longer felt. Love then ceases to be defined as "what is for *me* in this relationship; how much can I assuage my insecurity; how much physical pleasure can I derive from a certain conquest before I throw him/her by the wayside." Love becomes a service given without seeking attention or profit. At this point, one does not need injunctions like "Thou shalt not kill." The natural inclinations change, and one says, "I can no longer respond to violence with violence." "I simply cannot utter a false word, it just won't come out of my mouth." In the presence of such a person, violence ceases and thousands flock to him in complete trust. These principles of moral conduct and a well-disciplined personal life are the first two rungs of the ladder of yoga, called *yamas* and *niyamas*, well known to the students of this philosophy.

It is understood that people have different levels of energy, capacity and inclinations and cannot be expected to practice the disciplines in equal strength. The teacher waits patiently, but he also constantly coaxes, critizes, corrects because it is said in the texts, "Glory does not attend upon a man who has not exhausted all his efforts."

Physical Training: Hatha Yoga

This most well known part of yoga is often taught as merely a series of physical exercises almost completely divorced from the psychological and spiritual philosophy. In the tradition itself, it is not merely a way of keeping the body trim and fit. A yoga position is not called an exercise but *asana*, a posture. In a yoga posture, the body, breath rhythm, nerves, brain and mind are all totally involved. While the body is going into a posture, the breath is being exhaled, inhaled or retained according to prescribed rules; the nerves, brain and the mind are each given an exercise to do at the same time. The mind may repeat a certain word, concentrate on an idea or contemplate certain philosophical truths. The practice of hatha is divided into many aspects. It is not our intention to give the reader a detailed training in these pages; only brief descriptions follow.

Disciplines and Controls

The exercises of discipline and control involve and affect various areas of the personality. The *asanas*, postures, are of two kinds, some for physical culture and health and some for meditational sitting. In addition, there are postures called *mudras* which are meant to influence the finer nerve channels and energy flows. One must also learn the *bandhas* or locks, namely finger lock for meditative posture and rectal, abdominal, neck and tongue locks for various breathing and concentration exercises. These are often described in various popular books on hatha yoga without explaining their finer applications, which must be learned from a spiritual master. The joints and glands exercises, the benefits of which are obvious from their title, are not known to most hatha teachers even though they are simple and effective preparations and complements to asanas and other parts of hatha.

Cleansing Exercises

These exercises, from simple to more complex, are used for cleansing and detoxification of the internal systems. Briefly, again, they are as follows:

Cleansing the nostrils and the sinus
   a)   Drawing water from one nostril and letting it flow out the other, or through the mouth.
   b)   Cleansing with a string drawn in and brought out in the same way.

Upper Wash, filling the stomach with warm water and vomiting.

Complete Wash, flushing the stomach, letting the water flow out through the digestive system.

Natural enema in which the water is not forced up but drawn in through muscle control.

Cleansing the bladder and the urinary tract, with liquids similarly drawn in.

These are used not only for health but also because the body and internal organs of a meditative person become very sensitive and do not tolerate the presence of toxic and foreign material which hinder the autogenic controls.

All these practices should be learned under a teacher; some of the more advanced techniques are not being mentioned here to prevent the readers from harming themselves.

Pranayama

The practice of breathing exercises should be divided into these categories and steps:

Learning to breathe properly for normal daily breath.

Lengthening the breath and the capacity of the lungs.

Practices preparatory to alternate breathing.

Alternate breathing for strengthening the nerves and purification of the energy channels.

Breathing exercises:

for prevention and reduction of the disorders of internal organs, nerves and the brain, such as high and low blood pressure and insomnia;

for relaxation;

for autogenic training and control of internal organs and functions such as heart, digestion, and pulse beat;

for changing the mood and creative processes of the mind.

Svara practices of respiratory rhythms come under another branch of the science, leading to a very subtle control of the currents and crosscurrents of life, and to the system of micro-astrology in which all celestial signs are in the internal states.

It is a fact of yoga science that one who knows the right ways of *pranayama* and *svara* is a master of both the science of living and the art of dying. Autogenic training is a part of this science and art.

Does everyone have to go through all these exercises and practices? The answer is certainly, no. The practices are given according to one's age, capacity, specific problems and disposition. The success depends on commitment.

Mental Exercises

No real dividing line exists between the physical and mental exercises. Whatever a man does is first done mentally. All controls, discipline and training depend on the mind. For the purpose here, we term those as mental exercises in which the body is taught to become still and motionless and the mind is given specific directions. These mental exercises are divided into: relaxation, concentration, contemplation, and meditation as process. Meditation as a goal, the state of *samadhi*, is supramental. These stages of mental exercises may also be explained as ways of going inwards

from the body: relaxation
through cognitive senses: concentration
through intellect: contemplation
through total mind: meditative process
experience of Total Consciousness: meditation as
goal.

Relaxation

The relaxation exercises are done in crocodile, corpse and sitting positions. Of these, the most effective and methodical ones are practiced in the corpse posture (*shavasana*). This is a natural follow-up to physical yoga. All sets of physical exercises end in corpse posture. In popular Western yoga schools it is common for the teachers to introduce the corpse posture and suggest relaxation. The methodical way of relaxation known to the tradition is not introduced; the yoga class ends. We begin at this point.

There are methodical ways of relaxing each muscle and joint and even internal organs. The method proceeds from simple exercises to more complex ones such as the "funeral procession"—not to be described here.

These relaxation exercises have been proven the sure way of inducing alpha brain waves. They are also used to reduce problems such as migraine headaches and insomnia. Laboratory experiments have proved the exercises effective for reducing blood pressure and even helpful for cerebral palsy. These tests have been made in well-known scientific institutions on both sides of the "Iron Curtain." One of the effects of all these exercises is an increase in body heat. It is thus that the great yogis in the Himalayan mountain ranges can live without much clothing even at the height of 14,000 feet. In a laboratory situation, patients suffering from headaches have been taught to increase the warmth in their fingers, making the blood flow towards the hands and away from the head.

The increase in body heat is not merely because of the altered state of blood circulation, but because relaxation is conservation, as tension is loss, of energy. Many people equate the alpha state with meditation, but it is merely a relaxed state of muscles, nerves and the brain.

A slightly more advanced series of exercises produces theta brain waves, which are associated with concentration, mnemonic improvement and creativity. A few worthy disciples then advance to the exercises which open the mind's gateway into the subtle body. How far the aspirant may advance depends entirely on his motives and goals.

Concentration

Concentration is not a state of tension and true concentration of mind can be achieved only in a physically relaxed personality. A tense person cannot concentrate. Only when one has learned to maintain an easy and steady posture, and has the body, nerves, brain and the mind relaxed, can he begin to concentrate. In fact, relaxation and concentration are intertwined; one cannot relax the muscles of the toe if he cannot focus the mind's attention to that part of the body. It is thus that some of the advanced relaxation methods become purely concentration exercises.

The practices of concentration are varied and extensive. Briefly, these may be divided as follows:
- Concentration on individual objects of senses
  Objects of sight such as:

> flower
>
> flame
>
> image of the guru
>
> image of one's chosen deity
>
> a diagram
>
> a point, in different colors
>
> sun, moon, stars and so forth.

- Concentration on sounds such as
  > a single note from an instrument
- Concentration on objects of taste, touch and smell
- Concentration on earth, water, fire, air, space
- Concentration on a point of one's body, with or
  without
  > an object
  >
  > an image
  >
  > a diagram visualized there
  >
  > on breath
  >
  > on a thought, such as a mantra.

A concentration is prescribed by the guru, based on:

> the needs of the individual personality, and
>
> to produce a desired effect,
>
> for a certain period of time.

Particular concentrations have particular methods and should not be chosen at random merely in a mood of adventurism. When the initiate has absorbed the full psychological effects and is able to maintain a given concentration for an indefinite period of time, the object and method of concentration are changed.

There are four stages to a concentration on an external object:

- Concentration on an object, such as a flame, placed in front.
- Concentration on the memory of an object, for example: when one is concentrating on the flame, one may close the eyes and continue to visualize the flame;
- Reaching a stage of development where the memory of the object may be reproduced at any time and may be maintained for any duration;
- Total assimilation of the object of concentration, so that the concentration is no longer on the particular object nor on the memory of it in the conscious mind. The subtle body gathers together all the finer aspects that go into the making of an object and reproduces for the mind the attributes of the entire genus as a mental quality. In other words, the subtle body projects for the mind:

> the object (*dravya*)
> its attributes (*guna*)
> genus (*jati*)
> its activity or movement (*kriya*)

in such a way that, say, the entire flame-principle of the universe is fully understood and realized, with all its attendant conditions, qualities, times, space, causes, sequence and effect. By understanding the whole of the

> significator
> significatum
> significance

>> of

>>> the word
>>> object and
>>> relationship,

the entire principle is controlled from the inner world.

The whole of the genus includes the parts and the particulars. The subtle genus is grasped by the intellect as the root of the parts and particular qualifications and conditions. Then a certain *siddhi*, mastery, is attained which to other eyes appears to be a miraculous power whereas it is merely a matter of controlling the gross object through the subtle principles.

Contemplation

Our conscious intellectual activity is discursive, verbal, dealing in dichotomies; it is not an experience of unity. Contemplation is the use of intellect to transcend itself for an experience of that level from which intellect itself arises. It starts with a discursive thought but finally the entire energy of the thought is absorbed into the inner personality; the thought ceases to be a thought and its signification becomes an experience of a state of consciousness. Intellectually, one might start with a definite formula, such as "I am a pure being." One may analyze it linguistically and psychologically and write a thousand volumes of philosophy about it; this is still an outward progression of thought. It becomes a meditation only when the entire linguistic analysis is reduced, rather concentrated, into the inner experience of purity. This method of meditation is used in Jnana Yoga, which is the path associated with the Vedanta philosophy.

There are the six *mahavakyas*, great sentences, which form the essence of the philosophy, practice and realization of Jnana Yoga. Tens of thousands of pages have been written in the Sanskrit language in the form of commentary on these six sentences in the past twelve centuries in India.   Those who wrote the commentaries are the famous jnana-yogis.   The purpose of their commentaries was, on one hand, to express their own realization arising out of the contemplation and secondly to assimilate that realization of the Transcendental to the empirical world of daily existence, based on the principles of relativity, the categories of logic and relationship to other sciences.   It will be insufficient for one to merely read the six sentences and fully grasp their purpose, without going through the practice of contemplation as taught in the monasteries.   Some of the texts and commentaries are not taught outside the monasteries.   A novice is given one of these sentences for contemplation, much as a mantra is imparted.   The sentences are quoted here only to satisfy the curious:

1) All this is Brahman (One Supreme Transcendental Reality) indeed.
   The passage in the *Upanishads* continues, "there are no 'many' here . . . he who sees . . . from death to death he travels who sees 'many' here."
2) Brahman is the pure Gnosis (*parajnana*).
3) This self (*atman*) is Brahman.
4) That thou art.
5) I am that.
6) I am Brahman.

This is the quintessence of the Vedanta philosophy, especially as interpreted by Shankaracharya in the 8th century A.D.

The greatest philosophers of India were the monks of the school of Shankaracharya and they gave birth to the most formal schools of Indian philosophy. In the Western universities of today, Vedanta is almost synonymous with Indian philosophy even though many other highly developed systems of thought are also studied. The Vedanta philosophers can be equated with the great Christian theologians such as St. Thomas Aquinas. The method of contemplation can be compared to what is called meditation in the Christian seminaries, where a spiritual guide advises the student to contemplate on a certain passage of the scriptures: "The Word is God . . . and God became flesh": what does it mean? The student is not being advised to undertake a linguistic or logical analysis, but to experience it as a truth. One of the greatest yogis of India, Raman Maharshi, has taught the contemplation on "Who Am I?" Trace the sources of this very thought within oneself and you may get to self-realization. The way of contemplation in yoga is mostly used by the monks of the Vedanta tradition. There are the six Great Sentences, such as "All This is Self," that are assigned by a senior monk to a novice, someone being initiated into monastic life. The novice contemplates these sentences according to prescribed methods. This Yoga of Intellect is called the End of Wisdom, Vedanta, because starting from intellect it transcends intellect, as conscious merges with the Superconscious.

V
Preparations, Problems and Results

As stated earlier, the mind is the finest manifestation of material energy. Its velocity is faster than that of any atomic particle, and its capacity almost touches the fringes of the infinite. It stretches from the peace, tranquility and purity of the spiritual self to the grossest manifestation of false identity and identification with the material world. It would therefore be wrong to think of the mind as something definable with a single sentence, but we can make an attempt at a brief definition. The mind is that modification of energy which serves as a means of contact between the spiritual and material, between the conscious and the unconscious, between the self and the non-self. Therefore, a little of the conscious and a little of the unconscious, of the spiritual and the material is combined in the force called mind. It speaks to the self the language of the non-self and to the non-self the language of the self. It brings to the self the information regarding the external cosmic realities and brings to the material world the benefit of the consciousness and a little touch of the infinite from the transcendental. So it sullies the curtains around the self, yet it purifies the material world. It is an instrument both of greed and surrender, of attachment and renunciation, of crime and poetry, of murder and blessings of eternal life through initiations. Without mind, it would not be possible for the physical personality to be made alive and aware and for the senses to act on one hand, and on the other, for the cognitive senses to carry experiences inwards and for the self to know it has a body. The mind, therefore, acts on many different levels in many different capacities fulfilling many needs and performing many functions. A meditative person learns to distinguish these functions and to control the services performed by the mind.

Mind being what it is, a person who is traveling the path of meditation as a process walks a little in the sun and a little in the shadow, experiences a little peace and a little agitation, a little calm and a little disturbance. Because most people start with the expectation of instant peace and the Buddha-like enlightenment, they are frustrated when they encounter the hurdles presented by the mind on the landscape of the consciousness. They become discouraged, look for alternate paths, or leave the search altogether. Yet others start with the expectation of experiencing dramatic colors, thunderous sounds, celestial music and altogether a sensational presentation. This is especially true of those coming from the drug culture. These and many other problems need to be solved even before one embarks on the path of meditation, for it is better not to start on the journey at all than to return from halfway to say that the path that was taken and the goal just do not exist because one did not reach it. It is

better, therefore, to start with the right preparation.
We have already spoken of emotional and moral
controls. The entire lifestyle, the way one handles daily
emotions and decisions of each moment determines the
content of the meditation. The attitudes, then, are the
right preparation. There is a large body of texts, oral
teachings, and the techniques of ashram discipline to
help cultivate the right attitudes; only some of these
can be mentioned here. The first fourfold series of
attitudes is called *Brahma-viharas*, playing in God. These
four attitudes are *maitri, karuna, mudita, upeksha*, re-
spectively, friendship and love, compassion, joy and
indifference. Love for the happy and comfortable,
compassion for those in pain, joy at seeing others grow
spiritually, and indifference to evil. When the life is guided
by a proper balance of these attitudes, it gradually evens
out the rough edges and what develops is equanimity,
contentment, and natural success without struggle.
However, a proper balance of these is difficult to obtain.
How can one be indifferent to evil, for example? This
indifference does not mean that one need not help the
victims of evil, otherwise he will be breaking the advice of
cultivating compassion. In other words, all these attitudes
must work in conjunction so that the ego can be slowly
and gradually whittled down and true consciousness
emerge in its place.

The preparation can be of many kinds: material,
social, spiritual; of place, time, and relationship. Above
all, one must recognize the need for self-purification, as
explained in the previous chapters. Some of the other

preparations are as follows:

Satsanga, the company of the wise and virtuous, those who constantly advise, encourage, criticize, and remind one of the goal he has set for himself. The Buddha regarded *Kalyana Mitra*, a good friend, as the first factor in spiritual progress. In the same category, comes the attendance of group sessions when one listens to the words of advice and meditates together in the company of others. The companion who does not encourage one to walk the spiritual path, to purify oneself, should be avoided even at cost of utter loneliness. Yet it is dangerous for a beginner to try to become a total hermit or recluse right from the start. Therefore, the right company should be cultivated.

Svadhyaya, the habit of reading inspiring stories of the sages who have reached the goal in the past, regular study of texts and scriptures are all absolutely essential.

Regularity and moderation. These are advised in order to harmonize all your systems with the physical and respiratory rhythms. Irregular and immoderate physical habits make the breath irregular, mind moody, and meditation interspersed with unwelcome thoughts. A meditator, therefore, should have a daily schedule and fixed times for the various physical activities and needs, including the toilet, shower, meals, naps, sleep and sex. If one is not inclined to discipline the entire life, then the meditational experiences will have no firm ground. The simple physical functions should be regulated. The first thing one should do upon waking is to immediately rise and be aware of one's meditational breath. The first action one should do is a bowel movement. One should also empty the bladder after waking from a sleep, after a meal, after a long meditation and after sex. A morning shower after the bowel movement and before meditation is strongly recommended. In India, everyone goes out to a nearby river for the daily immersion before sitting down for prayer and meditation on the river bank. If the meals are regular, the bowel habits also will become regular so that the breath rhythms are not affected adversely. In meditation, breathing becomes naturally slow and deep but if the digestive system is unclean and uncomfortable, it produces irregularity of respiration and the irregularity of respiration is almost synonymous with mental disturbances of one kind or another.

Attitudes towards objects.   Going through the daily fulfillment of physical needs should be made the vehicle of cosmic awareness. Do not just take a shower but feel the galactic flux manifesting itself in the flow of sacred Jordan, Ganges and all other mother-waters of the world. Feel also as if the waters of peace are flowing from your skull through the entire nervous system all the way into the extremities of your fingertips and toes. A sip of water should not only quench the thirst but also wash the impurities of the heart along the way. The warmth and calories of food should become libations into the prana fires. When one views the objects as messengers of cosmic forces beyond the manifest limitation in which they only exist, he naturally induces a mood that somehow transcends the mind's bondage to the immediate time and space. Living with this type of mood of sanctity, one finds that when he sits for meditation, he requires much less effort for the transition from the external to the internal.

Cleanliness and order in all matters is a great help in keeping the mind free of confusion. Clutter in your surroundings and in your affairs is a projection of a mind that has become a drawer for the uncatalogued miscellany of life. Sort out your surroundings and the mind, and let everything be in its place. Many people sit for meditation in surroundings where the clutter is the last thing they see when they close their eyes to meditate, the clutter enters the mind; when they open their eyes, the same clutter is scattered around.

Fixed Spot. It is strongly advised to set aside a fixed spot with a comfortable and firm cushion and a beautiful mat as a personal citadel of your peace. As you approach this spot with the intention of meditating, change your mood, lie down for a relaxation exercise and then occupy the meditation seat. No one else should sit on that seat. After some months of using the same spot for daily meditation, you will create there a very special but invisible imprint of your meditative personality. The association will become so strong that the mere fact of thinking about the spot, let alone approaching or sitting on it will bring a change of mood. It is for this reason that the ashrams and hermitages of great sages and yogis have become places of pilgrimage. It is even better if, like your sleeping pajamas, you can keep a separate set of clothing for meditation.

Fixed Time. Keep a fixed time for meditation in your daily schedule. Twice a day is even better. In your entire philosophy up to now, there is no meditative center to your environment with things of space and time, and, therefore, the mind observes no rhythms and no harmony. Your fixed hour of meditation is the note with which the music of your daily mental moods should begin and with which it should end.

Posture. Like the meditation seat and fixed time, one should cultivate a fixed posture. The body and mind are inter-related—the body is the container and the mind is the liquid contents. Move the body and the mind loses its stillness. Initially it will be difficult to sit in the same posture for long, but there are ways of gradually lengthening the duration: preparatory physical yoga exercises, using will to overcome physical sloth, sluggishness and rigidity of limbs, relaxing the limbs, withdrawing the mind from the joints which hurt, concentration on breath and the mind's absorption into the depth of meditation. These are the steps in this very order, which will help prevent the body from becoming an obstacle in the way of meditation. Let the feet fall asleep so that the mind may wake to a new consciousness.

Guru Puja. Guru is the greatest secret in the tradition of Superconscious Meditation. Guru is not a person but a force-field and the person of the human Guru is only a point of focus. The true meditation is not developed by one's effort alone but by the Guru's transferring a little of the experience of his own consciousness to the disciple. As the meditator progresses under guidance, this fact of the Guru's grace becomes gradually clearer to him and it deepens his faith. When starting to meditate, pay homage mentally to the long line of Gurus of the tradition, thus placing your mind at the disposal of their grace. Empty your mind with an exhalation so that it may be filled during inhalation. Follow the method prescribed by the teacher. Do not mix methods of two teachers, though you may read and listen to all. At the close of the meditation, seek no results, expect nothing and mentally recite the formula "this meditation I surrender as an offering to the Supreme Reality and I lay no claim to any return."

Some people meditate with great expectations, others compete with fellow seekers or wish to prove to themselves that they have accomplished certain things in their practice. This means that they have not learned the secret of surrender and that to them meditation is an action rather than a state of being.

Do not try. Trying and struggling to achieve a level of meditation always brings the opposite results. One cannot fall asleep beating a drum and shouting to oneself repeatedly, "I am determined to sleep." The states of consciousness can be changed only very gently. Let meditation seep through you like water into a rock, like the sound of a falling rose petal, like a baby's finger growing invisibly, like the sun's ray sipping a drop of water. There are no dramatic manifestations, just a slow and graduating transformation.

Avoid strong moods. Meditation is an experience of equanimity. It is a turtle withdrawing its limbs. In order to avoid ups and downs in meditation, the life must be made an example of evenness. The moods of anger, depression and passions, strong desires and strong disappointments should be turned down. As soon as you notice a strong mood coming on, think of your meditative experience, become aware of a center of consciousness within you and decide to surrender the fruits of all your actions. As the meditation progresses, the rush of the moods also slows down.

By following these prescriptions, the mind will slowly, ever so slowly, change its habits. If you look at your face in the mirror every day, you notice no change from morning to evening. But see it after five years—the face has changed. So it is with the personality; the changes occur gracefully, progressively; therefore, do not be impatient. Only let meditation be absorbed into your personality over a period of time, and soon someone will surprise you by saying that you have changed.

How necessary are all these preparations? The answer is that the gap between the conscious and the superconscious, between life and meditation has to be narrowed down. Meditation must permeate life. Then problems of life will cease to distract the mind in meditation. The preparatory prescriptions above are some of the steps in that direction. However, one must be flexible. He who cannot break the rules gracefully cannot keep them gracefully. When the necessity arises, the rules should be broken by the careful use of discretion rather than laziness and other weaknesses.

So far as the relationship of meditation to daily life is concerned, there are three types of people.

Let us say this by way of analogies. Melt some butter and throw it in ice water. It immediately congeals; it can be picked out of water without leaving a trace.

When the practice of meditation is kept completely separate, the mental and physical habits of daily life keep rearing their ugly heads during meditation; the ground is not firm; one may easily drop off from the practice, and very little peace and equanimity flow into life. One struggles with a conflict that appears to exist between the meditative and ordinary life. Slowly, however, a little of meditation begins to seep into the attitudes, habits, actions and reactions. It starts in this way: the aspirant leaves his meditation seat in an altered frame of mind and first only for a few minutes and then for hours there remains a feeling of completeness, self-dependence, self-assuredness, and the word spoken, the decisions made or the actions performed seem to come from a deeper center within himself. However, the strength wears off and the ordinary life engulfs the mind. This is like mixing oil with water; it is neither quite well-mixed nor completely separate.

The next desirable state is of water and milk which, mixed, cannot be separated. The quality of life is so elevated that meditation becomes the very life. It permeates every act; every word is spoken from a spiritual depth. At this point, the student becomes a true teacher. He knows the currents and cross-currents of his own life and that of others and in the words of Guru-dev Swami Rama, "He sees in the subtle world six months ahead of what is to appear in the gross visible world." He is then a *videha*, the formless spirit, merely living in a body, but with no desires and passions of the body affecting the mind. He has risen beyond personality and chooses to project whatever personality will fit a given situation for the benefit of others. His behavior seems enigmatic in the eyes of the others ; but then, how many ants can map the anatomy of an elephant?

At this point, he does not go into or come out of meditation, rather from his spiritual center he goes out into the world to help and comes back into meditation. Even this is a lower step. The final rung of the ladder is that, when one stands on a rooftop surveying the landscape around and as a master of it all, he no longer moves through the changing kaleidoscope of moods and sceneries. He neither comes nor goes. This is called Self-realization, liberation. If you start your meditation with this alone as your goal, you will progress. If you resolve before starting your practice, "I have no interest in anything except the Buddhahood," then your meditation will prosper and the waters of the clear spirit will wash your stains, heal your pain as you grow. But for many, all this is too distant a dream. Let us therefore deal with some of the simpler questions that are asked by beginners in meditation.

I see many colors and faces, hear different kinds of sounds and voices of invisible masters, scenes and events come before my mental eye. Do they indicate my past lives, my future or present realities?

The thoughts and experiences in meditation arise from three sources: the memories and anxieties of the conscious mind, the distortions of the subconscious, and the deeper realities of the centers of consciousness. One of the greatest dangers for meditation is to take every internal experience as an experience of eternity. Often the people who are inclined to a life of fancy or imagination use meditation as an escape into a world of fiction, which is better left for the poet and the novelist. The best attitude to take about these experiences is to just notice them and then ignore them completely. If a certain experience becomes recurrent, then it is better to consult your spiritual guide, the teacher who has the experience and expertise to sort out as to what is arising from which levels. Otherwise you are more likely to get bogged down in the mire of fancy than to dive into the clear lake of the Superconscious. This is one point where the yoga term "superconscious" differs in meaning from its Jungian interpretation.

I hear so much about meditational experience but nothing ever happens to me. Is something wrong with my meditation?

Congratulations that you are free of all these interferences! If you are looking for flashing, colorful lights, go downtown any Saturday night. If you like thundering sound, stand by any highway. Meditation is not a melodrama or a theatrical performance. The only effect you should look for is an experience of stillness, first gradual and then absolute; the relaxation of the body, silence of speech, evenness of breath, tranquility of mind and the feel of an energy force within you, the life force and the consciousness force. It is a state in which you forget even the existence of your body, while enjoying the fullest alertness of the mind and heightened awareness of consciousness. When you open your eyes from such a meditation, you are surprised that you are sitting on a seat and that the variegated world of objects is still around you.

That sure is very encouraging; I want to get there fast. But how?

There goes your ego again. There are only three ways to get there: patience, patience, patience. The moment you are impatient, you recognize the force of time that places in your way the obstacles of space, and starts a new chain of causation. If you have not purified your emotions, the lightning rod of spirituality will only shock you rather than illuminate you.

What about things such as candles and incense for concentration?

Even the word God is not necessary, for Godliness is not in words, and a scientifically-minded atheist can meditate and come to an experience of inner peace which he may not choose to call by the words such as Divine or Heavenly. If, however, you are in a tradition or in tune with a philosophy of life where external objects may be used for sublime purposes, then a shrine, an altar, a picture of the guru or deity, the flowers, incense, and candles all fit into place. These and the sounds of spiritual music and chants full of meaning and subtle vibrations can help to calm the conscious mind, raise it to sublime levels and

induce a mood that leads to meditation. Although at some
stage, all these ritualistic props too will be left behind, if,
at the present level of your response, your spirit seeks this
type of environment and practice, be sure to ask your
meditation teacher for guidance. If she or he is well-
trained in the tradition, you will be given guidance
concerning the tested formulae and forms of meditative
worship that have been used for centuries in the yoga
tradition.

VI
Problem Thoughts in Meditation

Unless one knows the problems that arise on one's path, one cannot remove their causes and cannot remedy their effects, cannot prevent their arising and is unprepared if not expecting them. These obstacles arise in the way of almost everyone no matter how well refined his/her personality may be. The major problems are as follows:

Illness: The result of previously performed wrong karma, because of which one forgets the correct relationship between the self and the body. As a result of this, the *buddhi* or faculty of discrimination loses control, and one performs immediate acts which are harmful both to the body and the mind. The illness is an imbalance of the three humors: air, bile and phlegm. This imbalance causes a further imbalance in the seven components of the body; in the secretions such as glandular and digestive, blood, skin, marrow, bones, fat, and sexual fluids; as well as in the various senses. Unbalanced and immoderate habits of food, sleep and sex as well as unnecessary mental disturbances cause the imbalance of the humors and the resultant illness.

The mind's laziness: Even though one is willing, yet he does not undertake the practice or through negligence practices irregularly and infrequently.

Doubt: Expressed as to whether I will be able to practice or not; and even if I practice, would I ever accomplish anything; or, is there any good to the practice of meditation at all, would some other way be better?

Physical   and   mental   heaviness: Due to the imbalance of phlegm, etc. in the body or to the excess and predominance of *tamas* in the mind results in meditation being slothful.

Further problems arise
when the mind remains drawn toward the senses and their objects even during meditations;
through various kinds of mental obstructions the meditation does not come to any higher plateau;
even when it does come to a higher plateau, it does not stay there for long.

One experiences all kinds of pains and pangs, sorrows and griefs, as well as fears and physical obstructions and unnecessary agitation.
anxiety and frustration in the mind
unsteadiness of limbs
unsteadiness of breath

And all these can be overcome only through patience and regular practice.

There is a further division of the kinds of thoughts that arise in the mind during meditation because they are the normal tendencies of a person in life.   These are termed *nivaranas* or hindrances:

sense desires
ill will
sloth and torpor
restlessness and worry
doubt

Some schools are of the opinion that all other obstacles arise out of these five only. One has to work at gradually diminishing all these obstacles and hindrances and coverings of the mind.

The meditator is advised in all schools of meditation to aspire to practice four stages of thought, both in meditation and in life. These are:

1) wrong thoughts that have arisen should be made to cease,

2) wrong thoughts that have not yet arisen should be prevented from arising,

3) right thoughts that have not yet arisen should be made to arise,

4) right thoughts that have arisen should be maintained, strengthened and cultivated.

Why do all different kinds of thoughts arise during meditation? How do I prevent them?

This is the most common question the novices in meditation ask, and here we shall have to go into some detail. We have spoken above of the raw material of thought being a reflection and reaction; that reaction arises from the amalgam, the multicolored solution that is smeared on the face of the mind, distorting the reflections that fall on that mirror. When the thoughts arise, do nothing with them. This is the precise answer. The thoughts do not arise from anywhere but from within yourself. Every object has two aspects, material and mental. The material aspect is observed by the mind; the mental aspect is observed by the witness, that is, the self. In wakefulness we are most concerned with the material aspects and the mental reactions to those aspects. There is continuous reflection and reaction, a process of stimulation and response. As one is reading this book, there are many thoughts arising in the mind. There is a stimulus through the eyes and response from the mind. At the same time, many other little processes of stimulus-response pattern are continuing. There is probably an experience of the touch of clothes on the body. If you have not rinsed your mouth since your last tea, perhaps you have a little residue of taste in the mouth. Many people sit down to meditate without a physical preparation: without rinsing the mouth; without washing feet, hands and face; without cooling the neck; and wearing unnatural fabrics which produce all kinds of sensual stimuli on the skin. And then they say, "I am restless." Many people also sit down to meditate with worries and anxieties in their minds, so naturally different types of stimuli as well as mental conditions and preconditions produce thoughts.

As soon as one withdraws from the thought of the environment as well as the sounds and sights, he becomes aware of the body. And if the seat is not properly prepared, if the clothing is incorrect, if the body has not been cleansed, all these things, then these sensations are experienced. The body then begins to feel an itch, for instance. This reminds us of the story of a blind man who was left in a room and told to find the door by touching the walls. But a chemical had been sprayed on his body so that he continuously scratches. So he goes around and around in the room alongside the wall, but each time this terrible itching causes him to scratch with both hands and he misses the door! So, unless the body is well-prepared, through the practice of *hatha*, correct posture, and unless there is a correct and proper kind of seat and so forth, the body will never settle down. If the body is not still, the mind will not rest. There is a tradition in Raja Yoga that if one can sit absolutely still for three hours and thirty-six minutes, he/she will reach the state of *samadhi*. But it is not possible for an average individual to accomplish this without a great deal of preparation.

Physical conditions such as a heavy stomach, muscular strain and so forth cause further problems. Incorrect posture causes unnecessary pain in the ankles and knees. These problems can be overcome by the practice of methodical relaxation taught in the tradition. The mind should be trained to slowly slide away from the areas of pain and discomfort. Only after the physical preparations are complete can the mind learn to become still.

A still mind is not an empty mind. If one does not know what to do with the mind, the sensory deprivation caused by closing the eyes and ears can only be uncomfortable at best and can, at worse, even cause uncontrolled fantasies and hallucinations. A number of psycho-physiological experiments with sensory deprivation have proved this. The subjects were placed under conditions of sensory deprivation for a prolonged period of time with eyes sealed, no tactile stimuli, no sounds fed into the brain and so forth.   When all input is thus stopped, the mind loses hold of all things that it depends upon through habit in order to keep its balance.   Think of it this way: the mind has, as it were, lines and hooks reaching out through the eyes, ears and other senses, and in this way it holds on to a material, empirical reality.   When these hooks are suddenly removed and the strings suddenly cut, the mind is, as it were, in a dark chamber, feeding upon itself, upon its own memories, trying to derive raw material of thought from within itself.   It becomes the worse kind of cannibal, gorging upon his own limbs.   This should be prevented at all costs.   It is for this reason that in the practice of Superconscious Meditation the objects of thought are not suddenly removed.   Until one is capable of experiencing the *asamprajnata samadhi*, the highest state of consciousness of the Transcendental Reality, the mind should be given an *alambana*, a support, something to lean on, something to depend on, something to keep hold of, something to grab onto.   The mind is then *ekagra*, one-pointed, and not *niruddha*, ceasing all waves.   It is clear, therefore, that sensory deprivation alone will not still the mind, it may even agitate the mind further.   Just closing the eyes and ears and stilling the body but leaving the mind unprepared will not invoke a state of meditation. For this reason, the mind is given some object to concentrate on, whether it be a specific light or a sound, or a *chakra*, center of consciousness, but first of all a *mantram*, so that the mind may be filled with that one object, word or sound and have some one point to remain attached to instead of becoming a boat without an anchor in a stormy sea, very far away from the shores of external reality that is experienced through the senses. Thus the mantra becomes an anchor as well as a wharf, an anchor in the sea of meditation, a wharf in wakefulness. You see, you can prevent the monkeys of sense from seeing, hearing and speaking evil; but as soon as the eyes, ears and mouth are closed, the monkey that is mind will begin thinking all evil indiscriminately. In a state of artificial sensory deprivation when the mind has not yet learned to free itself from dependence on the objects of senses, as soon as an *alambana,* a support, such as the mantram is withdrawn, the mind begins to produce all kinds of images, thoughts, words, and associations, and one begins to see fearsome scorpions and spiders crawling all over inside the cavity of the skull!

The thoughts arise in the mind not from outside, but because they are present in the mind, both as potential in the raw material of memory and the subconscious, and on the conscious surfaces, whatever you have stored in the jar will be seen when you lift the lid. It is like a person who uses a large can to put his garbage in day and night. After many years of this, a visitor tells him that he has some precious diamonds at the bottom of the can. The person begins to search for these diamonds, and, as he puts in his hand, what he finds all the way through is garbage. He keeps his hand in the garbage for five minutes and, becoming despondent, withdraws the dirty arm and says, "I shall look for diamonds again tomorrow." But for the next twenty-three hours and fifty-five minutes, he continues to pour more garbage in that very can. Again, next morning he looks for the diamonds for five minutes and then continues to throw some garbage in. If, for twenty-three hours and fifty-five minutes a day you add to your mind all the confused and involved complexities of relationships, reactions and anxieties, then in five minutes of meditation you will come face to face with those very things. To purify meditation, purify life. Many people are afraid to meditate for fear of these thoughts arising. But sometimes they manage to overcome their fears and say, "Well, maybe there are diamonds there, and if there really are diamonds, I am a rich man; I'll try it." So they look inward and find what they have placed in the mind all the twenty, thirty, forty years of their life indiscriminately. But thank God these thoughts do arise because through them, if you are wise, you become aware of the content of your mind and you see what level of purification you have to work for. The random thoughts arising in meditation should be regarded as part of a purge and you can aid the process of the purgation as soon as you become aware of the presence of an undesirable thought.

There are five stages of the thoughts arising in the mind during meditation. Let us study these step by step.

The first stage is of random thoughts. A person has not learned to control his mind, so when these thoughts present themselves in meditation, he lets them carry him away. They start forming chains of thoughts. Through a process of free association, an image forms in the mind and leads to another image. A word arises and a sentence is framed and an argument begins. And carries on. One thinks of a blue shirt, then a friend who wore that blue shirt, then of a Cadillac, then the means of obtaining such a Cadillac, and before one knows, one is not in meditation but running a chain of supermarkets. One opens the eyes and he is right on his meditation seat. A doctor starts thinking of rich patients, a psychologist begins to psychoanalyze, a housewife quarrels with her husband, the husband fights with the wife, and a disciple often has long arguments with the teacher, right there in meditation. One often uses these meditation sessions for wish-fulfillment almost like dreams. Sometimes these daydreams and fantasies are of a very *tamasic* nature, dark, dull and depressing, and you become afraid and want to stop meditating. Sometimes they manifest *rajasic* tendencies, the novice becomes excited, agitated, restless, angry, or even sexually aroused. Sometimes they are of a *sattvic* nature, or a mixture of any of these categories.

Many times these daydreams and fantasies are mistaken for real experiences, works of intuition, revelations, messages from the teacher and masters; one visualizes oneself becoming a great teacher and teaching a crowd of ten thousand students, or prophesying the fate of the world, or seeing everybody's mind very clearly. Once someone called me in the middle of the night and said, "Panditji, in my meditation I have just received your message that I will be your successor to carry on the work in Minneapolis." I told him that my successor would be chosen by my own Guruji. I never saw that student again. A woman thinks that her husband who is not meditative will one day see a great light on her face and will be so impressed that he will become converted to meditation. Such powerful fantasies, weak fantasies, chains of thoughts, should be carefully watched.

They arise from the same amalgam, the same solution that is smeared on the surface of the mirror of your mind. How to control them? Does one fight them? The answer is, just ignore them. Observe that they arose and then turn your mind away from them. Just pay attention to the process of your meditation, "Mantra, arise; Guru, take over my mind; self, surrender." As soon as you become aware of an undesirable thought, do not let it become the start of a new chain, cut the link right there and go back to meditation. Just take note of the fact that such a thought arose, but do not let it propagate itself and create new thoughts.

Random thoughts always mean a tense body, and a tense body means random thoughts. Each is a correlate of the other, and it is not possible for one to be without the other. If you really want to handle these thoughts, immediately relax your body again and let your breath slow down. On the other hand, if you have difficulty relaxing your body, let your mantra arise in the mind and the body will slowly relax. But this fact must be remembered, that in the early stages of the process of meditation there is a mutual interdependence between meditation in the mind and relaxation of the body. So to handle these random thoughts and to prevent the chain from going on, in brief, take three steps:

   ignore the random chain of thoughts and fantasies,
   immediately relax all the muscles and joints with slow breath, and
   let your mantra arise in the mind.

Gradually, less and less of the chains of thoughts, fantasies and false visions will arise.

The second stage is that the random thoughts arise but no longer produce chains of further thoughts. The seeds sprout but do not become plants or trees. Something that was lying suppressed and dormant, comes now to the surface and evaporates, exhausting its energy very quickly. It dissipates its force and then no longer remains in the soil of your subconsciousness to produce further ill effects. This is one of the ways in which the hidden *karma* is reduced and the momentum of *samskaras* is exhausted. One should not rest contented at this point but observe each thought arising.

The first and the second stages do not have a clear demarcation line between them. Sometimes the student comes to the teacher and says, "I think I am getting much worse than I was. I have many thoughts arising in the mind. I have become more proud, jealous and angry. I observe in myself a certain streak of malice that was never there before." The teacher reassures the student that this is not really the case. These habits of malice and anger were there all the time but his mind was so bound to the things external that he had never quite come face to face with his personality. Just as one develops the expertise in observing the random thoughts in meditation, one also observes the habits of one's mind in daily life. He becomes aware of the various streaks of his own character and aspires to purify them. He wants to improve his relationships with others; wants to practice the *yamas* and *niyamas* much more intensively; wants to become a better person overall and observes his actions with great care.

This leads to the third stage of development. The thoughts intervening in meditation will not be general and random but very specific, dealing with practical problems, with what your conscious or subconscious mind is particularly occupied with at that time. This will show the seeker the real level of his life from which he has to learn to rise. He must replace these negative thoughts with positive attitudes and cultivate these attitudes. This is not, again, totally an undesirable state because it shows him if he has really learned to read his thoughts in meditation, at what level he is really operating, and what are the true conflicts of his personality behind the facade of a pleasant face and polite conversation. These thoughts are the measuring devices that tell him of his progress or lack thereof.

Not only the conflicts of life appear in the mind awaiting an inner solution, but also a conflict between life and meditation may develop. I aspire for greater meditations, to spend more time on it, but my husband or wife does not appreciate the time I spend in this practice. I would like to reduce my commitment to the economic pursuits; how can I accomplish this so that I may spend more time meditatively? Such problems of conflict arise and there are two ways to handle them.

One, the aspirant should learn to take the effects of his meditative experience into life as an aid to greater peace and tranquility in his relationships. The dichotomy between life and meditation should be resolved. Instead of rising in meditation and leaving life behind, one must raise life to the meditative level so that the gap, the difference of levels between the two, is reduced.

When the mind is elevated and the inner personality is transformed, the attitudes towards life also change. Such a change brings harmony in all actions and interactions. There remains nothing to be achieved by such a tranquil mind. When the inner conditions are transformed, naturally the conflicts are removed. No more does the external world become a source of obstacles and the adjustment becomes easily spontaneous. It is not necessary to change the relationship but to change one's attitudes guided by a meditative and tranquil mind.

A meditator should transcend his inner personality instead of trying to change others or expect others to change for him. Such a notion could be the projection of ego creating conflict more and more at home and outside.

It must be remembered that in any relationship, you are half the factor. The problem is often not in the person but in the way the relationship develops as a result of the wrong mode of thought. One example will suffice. At the Meditation Temple in Minneapolis, the earlier group of people was of young seekers who turned away from the drug culture to come to the practice and philosophy of meditation. Their constant complaint was about the suspicion of their parents: "We would very much like to involve our parents, but they are of a generation that doesn't care about these things," was the comment. After a while, the older group of doctors, psychologists, businessmen began to join the meditative life. The complaint of this group was that they would very much like to involve their children, but the younger generation doesn't care for such disciplines! The two groups seem to function each in an orbit of its own, and until the momentum of previous relationships and attitudes is exhausted, until the preconditions of mind have been cleared away through meditation, the two generations will not meet. The problem is in neither generation but in the attitudes.

The mind looks for external excuses, the teacher replaces a father figure, and we do not like meditative disciplines because we did not like the fatherly disciplines. We want to be guided, but do not want to be advised. Until the mind has given up this habit of looking for excuses from outside, it will never resolve the conflicts within. The conflicts concerning life will make themselves felt in the mind and will befog the meditative levels. A stronger soul resolves the crisis, makes a choice and sticks to it, or merges the momentum from two forces and makes the enemy into a friend. There are not clearcut solutions, definite answers, recipes or prescriptions, and no amount of advice from the guru will help you there. Do not expect the guru to be a psychotherapist, to analyze your daily emotions. Make your choices through free will, a will free of the bounds of your personality, a will free of the external circumstances. A will subject to the vagaries of the subconscious is not free will.

Here you face the problem of choices in life, your future course of actions, and until your choices are clear, the problem thoughts in meditation will continue. At this point, many people turn away from the spiritual life or hesitate for many years or months. Learn to resolve the crises of life by making your own choices very clear to yourself, become aware of your goals and your values. What is it that you are looking for in life? Are you a race horse that can beat every other horse to the finish line? Or are you on your way to becoming a meditative saint? Most people lead the lives of race horses, wanting to beat every neighbor to the finish line, whatever that finish line may be. Perhaps it is merely a director's chair in the office, or it is a matter of having one up over your husband or your wife. These things are not in consonance with any spiritual goal or aspiration. Find out why, then, you are tempted towards them. What are your resistances?

These problems may be divided into temptations and resistances:

1) You are drawn to some things which are opposed to meditative life, and

2) You resist things which support the meditative life.

These temptations and resistances come in your way because of your false identification and your false ego. Here you are referred back to the series of squares on page 22. These temptations and resistances arise in meditation in spite of your aspiration to have a purer experience. The moment you settle down on the meditation seat and begin to repeat the mantra in the mind, the disturbing thoughts arise. Your mind is a stage and the theatrical performance begins with dramatic exchanges: "Oh, that person! Did you ever expect this from him? How much I helped him! How unfair he is. Next time I meet him I will tell him this or that! How shall I tell him off? He is causing so much damage!"

"No. No. I should not have these thoughts. I am meditating. Mantra, begin." The breath slows down, the mantra repeats a few times. Then, after one minute, "He is awful, isn't he?"

"No. Mind, come back to meditation!" You come back to meditation and after a minute again, "She used to be such a sweet person when I married her. I don't know what has happened to her these days."

So you have half a minute of meditation and one and a half minutes of fight, then twenty seconds of meditation and two minutes of wrestling, and that fight and wrestling is the resistance, creating an obstacle in the way of your progress. But, did that other person do that much harm? And how did his act concern you? Even if he only has added all the *rajasic* and *tamasic* elements into the situation, would you let those elements come from the situation into your personality? She, the other person, had those thoughts and spoke such words; fine! She added darkness to her spiritual life; but why should you allow that darkness to be poured into your self? If a neighbor gives you a gift, and you do not take it, it no longer belongs to you and is of no concern to you. If you give a gift to someone at Christmas time, you do not drop in at his home at Easter and say, "I have come to see how you are treating my gift, whether you are keeping that shirt laundered, or that coat repaired." It is no longer your concern. If the person spoke hurtful words, between that person's mouth and your ears is a distance of perhaps six feet or more. But what is the distance between your ears and your mind? Let that distance grow. Let it become a distance of infinity for the inner space is infinite. Do not let those words travel from your ears into your mind. Let them slide off the surface of your ears, let the unpleasant sight drop off from your eyebrows to the ground, leave them there scattered and walk away free.

Here, you must ask yourself, not what is it in that person that I am resisting, but what is it in me that is resisting? When some of these angry, hurt, frustrated thoughts arise in meditation, right there in the meditation, look for their sources within. What part of your ego is resisting that person, that situation. It is clear that very few people ever do manage to do really any serious harm to you. Then what is it in your mind that is disturbed? One part of your mind will say, "Well, he just is bad," or "She just is terrible." How does that evil affect you, you who are here and not over there with them? Slowly, another layer of your mind comes forth and says, "Well, I have had my pride hurt by him; I want to make him feel that I am bigger than he." As soon as this happens, you reach a conclusion about yourself that you will not want to face. Many excuses will present themselves. When you face this, you will feel somewhat guilty. A *little* guilt is an excellent instrument of purgation and purification. If you recognize that the brakes or steering of your car are not working well, you also recognize that you have not taken good care of them. But at this point, you normally do not just sit by the roadside and feel guilty; you take necessary action to have them repaired. So, as soon as you come face to face with your ego, in search of those aspects of your personality that are resisting in a situation, be completely merciless with yourself. Recognize that you have to work in sun and rain to get your brakes and steering fixed. You must be prepared to go through a little pain, a final burst of pain, to burn off that wart of ego. Whenever you fail spiritually, recognize the failure, know that you have what it takes to make yourself a success, take the correct steps of the process of purification of thought, and your mild guilt will become your friend.

Then wash off that mild guilt feeling and recognize that you have been trying to show off your pride to the person who has been contesting that pride. As soon as you have this fresh evaluation of the situation within your self, about your self, you will experience a hot, searing pain. It is better for you to go through that half a minute of pain than to leave these *samskaras* lingering to create further festering swamps in the subconscious, producing the momentum of events in a different direction. This searing pain will burn the momentum of this particular situation; it will burn a part of your karma through right knowledge about yourself and, after that half a minute of painful burning of ego, you will go into a quieter, clearer meditation.

Henceforth, you will not react to that situation from the basis of the data, impressions and experiences you gather from without. You will act dispassionately. Next morning, you will wake up and out of nowhere some thought will arise in your mind to guide you. Either in meditation or even in the middle of ordinary movements of the day, your mind will say, "When I speak to that person, I shall use such and such positive phrases." These phrases will definitely elicit a positive response; but even if they do not, your agonies will have ended. The external situations will have ceased to internalize in you and your mind will be clear like a flowing river water. You have passed the most difficult stage of the problem thoughts in meditation.

In the fourth stage, the problems arise very seldom but answers, solutions and guidelines begin to appear. A little incomplete poem will be completed. The teacher will receive a new lecture, or a dictum. A forgotten verse will be remembered, the plan of a project will flash in five minutes and in this way, the meditative state will become the guide for a successful and prosperous life.

Again, there is a great danger that you may not be able to recognize whether you are passing through a process of wish fulfillment, subconscious motivation in disguised form, or whether it is truly the spiritual will of the superconscious using your conscious mind as its instrument. But soon you will begin to discriminate between the two sources and your life plans will become clear to you as manifestations of the divine will. Now your ego will tell you that you are a great man. The moment that such a thought enters, that you are a great man, a purified soul working for God like a divine messenger or a prophet, do not let God become the instrument of your pride. After you are through with the day's meditation, you may note down the solutions and the directions and establish your relationships on the basis of an egoless concern for the spiritual progress of others. One of the perfections required of a potential Buddha before reaching buddhahood is *upaya-kaushala*, an expertise in the means of liberating others. This is very patient work for your progress and for that of others.

In the fifth stage, no thought arises uninvited, you know how to let the superconscious speak to you. The details of the fourth and the fifth stages are to be reserved for personal teaching to be given by a teacher to a close disciple only.

VII
Ways of
Deepening Meditation

It is human nature to pursue pleasure. Unless one looks forward to the practice of meditation as pleasant, unless one ceases to think of it as a forced discipline, he cannot develop a positive attitude without which many kinds of resistances will develop blocking the progress toward deeper meditation. It should be remembered, therefore, that there are two kinds of pleasure. Pleasures of excitation and pleasures of tranquility. The pleasures of excitation are well-known to everyone: surfing, sexing or mountain climbing, tasting a delicious dish or taking LSD are all pleasures of excitation. In these there are hills and valleys, waves and troughs; a pleasure of excitation lifts you up and then drops you down, it exhilarates and then depresses, it refreshes and tires. It uses up energy and leaves behind exhaustion. The higher the mountains of excitement, the deeper the valleys; going up and coming down.

The pleasure of tranquility is that of a deep sea diver. Fifteen feet below the surface, there are no stormy waves and there is true communion with the spirit of the sea. Meditation alone is the pleasure of tranquility. In this there are no exhilarations and excitations but a calmness, leaving behind no depressions and no exhaustions. Look forward to this meditation, to this pleasure daily, and slowly it will cease to be a discipline. You will then learn to drift slowly into it as you do into deep sleep and the depth will arise to meet you, the heights will come down to greet you, and you will be a free bird with balanced wings in heaven and earth.

Now to something more specific. In order to deepen one's meditation, it is essential to know the ways in which teaching and guidance in meditation comes down to us. A teacher employs many ways to guide a student. The student himself should employ many ways to guide his senses and the mind. The means that the teacher employs to guide you should be employed by you to guide the senses and the mind so that you gradually build up your mind to meditation. This will be done in several ways. One is that certain acts or words or guidances or thoughts prior to meditation build up a mood. The same acts and thoughts repeated often enough change the total content of your subconscious mind, thereby changing your inclinations so that you will become more inclined towards meditation. And in meditation itself fewer obstructions will appear. These acts may be done through the senses, not by totally withdrawing the senses from their objects as you do in meditation, but by limiting their experience to only those objects the thought of which will be helpful to meditation. This is again the principle of turning your enemies into your friends. These objects may be words, chants, pictures, concentrations,

prayers, ceremonies, anything. Take, for example, someone's mantra is *Govinda* and someone else's mantra is
Hari; someone's mantra is *Namah Shivaya*. There is often
a chanting of collective mantras before a group meditation. Why? Because there, then everyone takes an idea
and totally absorbs himself in it through sound and music.
The repeated action makes the idea and the psychic force
associated with the given sound sink into the conscious
and the subconscious mind.

Since our senses have the natural tendency to open
outwards, we use those enemies for friends. They have
been beguiling us long enough, so we are now going to
beguile them. Mind, do you like speaking? Then speak;
I shall not stop you from speaking. But let's join the
game and make a compromise: you like speaking and I
like deeper thought, so I shall give you a thought and you
speak it, sing it. That becomes a chant. Hands, do you
like moving, do you like holding and moving, I shall give
you an object, a *japa-mala*, beads to count the recitation
of the mantras. Mind, do you like thinking of water and
of flames? Then, let us change the meaning of the flame;
instead of you saying the word "flame," let us make it
a symbol of the light that comes into meditation. Let us
look at the flame; sit and gaze at it and let it become a
concentration. Some like to think of a flame in poetic
and inspiring surroundings, and it becomes their altar.
These are the gentle ways of diverting your senses without
their resisting you.

In the case of a chant, some mantras may be
collective, and you let your mouth sing them, absorbing

the sounds of others around you as well as listening to your own sound within yourself. Let your mouth sing the mantra chant, repeating the same thought over and over again. Slowly let the chant become softer, and it will lead you into silence of meditation. Some minds do not respond to a chant; for them there are other ways. A teacher stands, as it were, on a peak and can see from there all the forest trails and pathways coming up the hill and watches those who are climbing up each of those trails. His task is to help each one up his own particular trail without their cross-referencing or debating with each other as to the propriety of the path they have taken or have been given. A teacher will take one student through the path of a chant, another through the path of light, one through a ritual, another through science. He knows the map of those paths. But since you do not need any path other than your own, avoid all others, skirt them, take a detour and go your own way. Chant, do not chant . . . worship at the altar, do not worship at the altar . . . sing, do not sing . . . concentrate on a flame, do not concentrate on a flame . . . use scientific, rational method, use intuition. What to others looks like a contradiction, to the man on the peak looks like an additional way of climbing up the mountain.

There are many ways of supporting your meditation:

1) Personal meditation alone on your meditation seat at a fixed time.
2) Meditating with the family.
3) Meditating at the same time as a group of people of kindred spirit but not sitting at the same place.

Six people may agree among themselves to sit at the same time, each in his or her own home.

4) Meditating with a group sitting together, but without the teacher.

5) Meditating with a group under the guidance of the teacher.

6) Person to person meditating in the presence of the teacher.

A proper initiated teacher knows whether a student is meditating at a fixed time or not because he is sensitive to a certain field of silent, superconscious thought that is generated when people meditate. At that time, he too sends out a prayer through his line of gurus to God to help and guide you. It is a well-known feature in the yoga tradition that a teacher may, from a great distance, even awaken you from sleep if you are in danger of missing your meditation time.

When a person meditates alone, he learns to depend entirely on himself without seeking psychological support, and it strengthens him. This must be your normal procedure. When you meditate with the family, the collective *karma* and the collective *samskaras* of the family are purified together, and the entire family takes a single direction, sharing in the field of love that is generated. If a husband and wife meditate together or both meditate, even separately, their relationship with each other will definitely improve because during meditation many of their little, mutual blocks will be removed; and stains of the strains of relationship will be washed off. When they will arise from meditation, their words and voices to each other will be softer and the approach more positive. The children may learn to meditate with their parents from a very early age. Once they have learned to enjoy meditation, the practice can be used to calm them down when they are excited and they will also understand the importance enough so as not to disturb the parents' own meditation. To deepen your meditation, there is nothing like the entire family becoming meditative, not only because of the collective consciousness of the whole family working together, but also because a number of conflicts between meditation and family life will be reduced.

The same type of group consciousness principle applies to group meditations. When people meditate together, they generate a field, each member supporting others. The time for such a group meditation may be fixed among the members themselves, or by the advice of the teacher. This way, you also learn to surrender your individual freedom for the benefit of all, to join with them in what the Christians call "becoming limbs and members of Christ consciousness." The Guru Spirit will often transcend the barriers of time and space to help the consciousness of the group. This is also where the Christian term, "like the intervention of the saints," or the yoga term, "like the grace of the guru" become meaningful.

Not only the unity of consciousness principle is realized in a group meditation, but when such a meditation is conducted in the personal presence of the teacher, two more things happen. The guru guides in a relaxed and meditative voice because he himself speaks from within the depth of his meditation. If a teacher cannot go into deep meditation before guiding the group, he is not a fit teacher. But an expert teacher's voice and quiet manner help you at the level of perception through your eyes and ears. His stillness, again, rubs off on your spirit. Moreover, a properly initiated teacher also touches the fringes of your mind to nudge them a little to stillness, towards a deeper meditation. The same happens in a person to person meditation.

In a person to person meditation with the teacher, a specific technique suited for your practice is taught, and your mind is helped into gaining mastery of the particular technique. After a personal or group meditation with the teacher, you will find the disciples very soft-spoken, gentle of manner, because with the mind stilled, the desire to speak aloud and the desire to bring all the irritations to the surface just evaporates. Where a teacher is available, once a week meditation with the teacher in a group is highly advisable.

Now we come to your own personal practice apart from that of a group. The ways of progress may be placed under these categories:

Practice
Method
Sahaja
Initiation

Most beginners sit to meditate, say, fifteen minutes every morning. But they do not really meditate for those fifteen minutes, but rather only for perhaps two minutes. The rest of the time they ride airplanes, chase butterflies, go horseback riding and skiing, have sword fights with friends or arguments with the teacher. This is a common phenomenon and we have discussed earlier the ways of preventing this and going through it. Now you should lead yourself to this process in this way. An advanced teacher knows many different techniques; in fact, he should be proficient in the techniques of all the schools of meditation. He may even lead a class or a group through a variety of meditations for the purpose of demonstrating the wide scope of the science. But he will emphatically advise that you:

Use only a single method
> Consistently
> Punctually
> Regularly
> With depth of concentration
> Patiently
> For a long period of time

If you have been sitting for twenty minutes but actually meditating only two minutes, gradually increase the durations of actual meditation in each sitting from, say, two to three, four or five minutes.

Lengthen the period of each sitting gradually from fifteen to twenty to twenty-five minutes, and so on.

Increase the frequency of your sitting. If you sat once, now sit twice a day, doing the meditation at the right time, that is, at a fixed time if possible, unless sickness, travel, the presence of a young child really prevent it. Be faithful about the practice.

At whatever time and for whatever length you sit, learn to deepen the meditation. The more you will practice, the longer you will practice, the deeper your meditation will go.   Through the practice you will gradually reach a point, a plateau, that will become your normal ground.   As the difficulties present themselves in the process of reaching from one ground to another, the teacher's help and guidance should be followed.   When you have reached a certain plateau there is always a danger of slipping down.   Be patient if you feel yourself slipping down and continue the practice, and after a week or a month, you will begin to climb again.   Until such time that you never slip again from that particular plateau, continue the same practice.   Thereafter you will begin to take that plateau for granted and will reach it without any effort, and will start your practice from that point to climb upwards, and you will pass through the same process of facing and overcoming difficulties and falling and reversing the falls until the second ground becomes firm.

It is not important that you should have an advanced method given at every step, but rather that you advance within a method given and master it completely.   One of the greatest obstacles in the way of progress is impatience.   Many people have asked my Gurudeva: "I do not seem to be making any progress, do not seem to be getting anywhere."   And he asks: "Where did you expect to get? What did you expect to happen?"   If you had expectations, you were not meditating.   After hearing such questions repeatedly from a certain group, he asked a certain person, "How long have you been meditating?" And the reply was, "Perhaps six months."   "How long do you sit?"   "Twenty-five minutes."   "Do you manage to sit still?" He said, "Yes, I think so." Gurudeva said, "That's great. Six months ago, would you have thought of sitting still for twenty-five minutes? Why do you think you are not making progress?" The mastery of a particular method in meditation is judged in these ways:

1) I can sit still and enjoy sitting, which I did not in the beginning.

2) When I am sitting still, my body, mind and nerves are relaxed.

3) Fewer and fewer random thoughts, fantasies or false visions arise.

4) When these thoughts, etcetera, do arise, they are of gradually shorter durations and weaker intensity.

5) The mind is free of them for progressively longer and longer durations—to be counted initially not in hours but in minutes.

6) Consequently, I have a great feeling of quietness and stillness:
   (a) during meditation
   (b) after arising from meditation

7) After arising from meditation, my feeling of calm and peace, as well as my awareness of my breath and repetition of the mantra continue deeper and longer through my daily activities.

8) I reach a certain plateau much more quickly after sitting than I did before.

9) In my daily activities, I have the desire to return to meditation more often.

10) During my daily activities, my breath awareness,

mantra and meditative state, or just my poise and calm, returns to me frequently.

11) The depth I experience in the presence of a teacher when he is giving a group or person to person meditation, I begin to touch on my own and gradually without fail.

12) As my depth in meditation is increasing, certain guidance in establishing more peaceful personal relationships is taking place. My ideas of morality, violence, non-violence, diet and other areas of the life style are changing. I am undisturbed by little things and not overjoyed by small successes, achievements and little gains, nor am I depressed as often as before at little failures.

An additional test will be a reduced desire for and expectation of thrilling experiences, sights and sounds in meditation. The path of meditation is one of tranquility and calm and not of adventure trips. If you reach a state of tranquility and begin to grope for a touch of infinity, your meditation is succeeding. If any experiences come to you while you are following a certain path, take note of them as you take note of the landmarks when you are driving from one city to another. But you do not try to purchase every mountain or build a household in every valley or stop at each motel as you pass, nor does your method of driving change from village to village. So do not be over-anxious for more advanced methods. To receive a more advanced method, the first thing is to please and satisfy the teacher that you need and deserve his physical presence and he will arrange such special sessions for you.   But he should not become a prop; otherwise you will never accomplish anything on your own. For this reason, in order to maintain more self-dependence in you, the teacher will often appear indifferent, avoid and shun you, criticize you, or even discourage you with his actions if not with his words. With his acts, he is saying that you should continue to apply the technique he has already taught to the depth he has already shown and that meanwhile there is little for him to say.

Many students state that when they apply the technique themselves, they face many mental obstructions which are not present when they meditate with the teacher.   However, it is good that they come face to face with these obstructions, that they know that these problems exist.   Now the student's work begins in order to overcome them, befriend them, or replace them.   When you reach a certain plateau consistently and simply cannot go beyond it and the teacher has seen in you, in your ways of sitting, walking and speaking certain signs of improvement, he will naturally give you a more advanced method. Sometimes he will give you a glimpse of more advanced methods beforehand, but you should not follow them unless he personally instructs you to do so.   This is essential;   no matter in what books you read about what chakras, in what lectures you hear concerning certain concentrations, unless the instructor says personally: "Now you add this to your method . . . ." just continue with the practice originally given.

How did the ancient masters develop the methods

and how did they transmit them?   There are five stages
to observe concerning one's own meditations:

    1)   preparations for meditation
              environmental
              physical
              mental
    2)   the process of entry into meditation;
    3)   the experience upon reaching a plateau, and
           gradually making the ground firm;
    4)   the process of emerging from meditation by
           observing;
    5)   reflecting upon a previous meditation.

An average person is not trained to observe his own
mind or his own states of consciousness, but as the practice of meditation deepends, one gains deeper and greater
facility with this particular faculty. The teacher observes
exactly what happens to his consciousness as well as to the
correlative physiological states, from moment to moment.
The deeper the meditation, the finer the observation, so
that in the fifth stage, as above, one remembers the entire
process. When transmitted, this becomes a method. Since
the student has not yet done enough practice to reach a
higher plateau, he is taught to prepare himself. What
comes naturally to the teacher, comes to the student
through the repeated practice of the method given. This
brings us to *Sahaja*.

The Sanskrit word *saha*, with, within; *ja* comes from
the verb root *jan*, to be born. *Sahaja* is something inborn,
innate, natural. A method followed faithfully prepares
you for a *sahaja-dhyana*, spontaneous meditation, flowing

from within, leading to *sahaja-samadhi*, the highest state of consciousness coming to you. The purpose of the method is to reduce the resistance of the gross, more external, so that the finer, the more internal, may make itself felt. The ancient seers observed the way the states of consciousness developed in a *sahaja* way in them. They also found the resistance in the grosser levels of their disciples, so they taught the disciples to resist the resistances, to whittle them down gradually so that the inner, finer principles might take over. The method is like the cranking of an old car.

Sahaja is the switching on of the ignition from within. Discipline of practice is a training to gear and harmonize the external aspects of the personality, to listen to the call of something deeper within, so that the fine, subtle vibrations arising from within do not get muffled by the noises going on in our external senses and in the conscious mind. For example, the *mantram* is practiced at five levels. Initially, one has to sit down and repeat it, perhaps with the lips, counting the repetitions on the beads or on the fingertips. But when one reaches the state of *ajapa-japa*, recitation without effort, unrecited repetition is like the sound of a single hand clapping. The analogy is familiar to all the schools of meditation. The unstruck sound arises, the mental vibrations are felt, the external sound is not needed to induce the mental state, the mental state brings forward the *mantra* or a physical or respiratory condition. This is a special subject on its own and will be discussed in a more advanced text.

The *mantra* and *kundalini* initiations also shall be

discussed in another text. Suffice it here to say that an initiation is a deep experience given by a guru, showing to the disciple in advance what his goal is to be. A guru is one who can induce an initiatory state of consciousness in the disciple *without* any objective or physical means.

Now, some of the simple techniques of deepening the meditative practice that you have resolved to observe consistently, punctually, regularly, with a depth of concentration, patiently, for a long period of time:

- Do not go ambitiously and to the most complex parts of the technique. Work according to your capacity and start with the part which is simplest and easiest for you to practice. Hold your mind to that part of the practice and do not let it drift away.

- If you find the random thoughts arising, there is tension in your body and an unevenness in your breath. Check and relax the tense parts of the body immediately, make the breath even again, then turn the mind back to the method being practiced. The physical tension and random thoughts are permanent intruders. Break their association, and they will lose their strength.

- Understand the relationship of body and mind. All sense perceptions create sensations in the nerve endings hidden in the skin. These minute tensions are conveyed to the brain which naturally responds to these stimuli, in turn producing tension in the muscles and nerves. Meditation in its early stages consists of breaking the stimulus-response pattern. Cease stimulation from outside;

let the instruments of response not respond to the stimuli, and let the instruments of registering stimuli cease to send the signals.

• Understand the relationship of breath and mind. Let us illustrate with a simple exercise that any reader can try. Select a particular thought: a red rose, the face of a beloved, the name of a deity, or any other thought. Exhale and think that thought; inhale and think the same thought unceasingly. Keep doing this for a few breaths. Then, *not at the end of a breath but right in the middle,* try to switch the mind to some other word or thought . . . *without* breaking the breath. You will find this impossible to do, because the breath and the mind are interwoven. Once you understand this, you will have no difficulty mastering at least the beginning practice of meditation.

The random thoughts sneak into your skull while you are meditating. Do you have a hole in the wall, do you leave a door open through which they come? Yes, indeed, and the door is the space between the breaths.

> *Breathe slowly,*
> *smoothly, without a jerk;*
> *without pause between the breaths;*
> *abdominally, with the diaphragm pushing up*
> *against the lower lung;*
> *lengthen the breath, but not beyond your*
> *capacity; and*
> *keep feeling the touch of the breath against*

the mucous membrane in the nostrils, un-
ceasingly.

Follow these rules in conjunction with other parts of the practice given to you, and it is impossible that your mind will not settle down.

Here another practice may be prescribed to help deepen your meditation. Select a thought. It may be your mantra, the sacred name of your chosen deity, a sound combination given by the teacher, or it may even be just a thought you have noticed arising in your mind. Grab hold of this thought. Now, use your volition, and let your consciousness command your mind to introduce this thought into your brain. Do not let the brain send the message down the line of command through the nerves and muscles to form words in the mouth. Repeat the process of introducing the thought from volition and consciousness into the mind and then the brain. Repeat it and observe the process. Observe not from what corner of the skull but from what level of consciousness this thought is arising. Then repeat the thought while exhaling. Repeat it also while inhaling. Make sure to take it back to the original level from which it arose. Do this repeatedly and watch the exhilaration of your consciousness. There are many other variations to this technique.

Your teacher will give you further instructions, and if you are a serious seeker, he will give it for your whole life and even through the following incarnations. But for now, just master the simplest part of the method taught and that will open up the floodgates of further knowledge.

Many texts and teachers describe special postures and practices such as the anus lock and tongue lock. I find these distracting. Are they absolutely essential?

As is said above, master the parts that are the simplest for you, and practice the rest at your own leisure.

I think I will try these methods with determination.

Oh, no determination, please. Just a gentle resolve will do. To alter a state of consciousness by force is to shake a bud to burst into blossom before its time. Can you fall asleep with declared determination? You can only drift gently into it. Slowly perfect one ground, one level, until it becomes firm and then you will not have to reach out for the next. You will just gently drift into it. Surrender your lower to the higher and success is yours.

What is exactly meant by this word "surrender"?

The infant raises his arms, the mother picks him up. Purify your will, know your goal, be very certain about it, and your journey will be brief. You will be given a push all along the way.

There are two factors in the practice of meditation: method and the man. The man is the disciple and the guru is both. There are two ways of purifying life: acts and grace. There are two ways of deepening meditation: effort and surrender. The two are one. But if you have a conflict, then choose the man; God in the guru, His grace and your surrender. It is by surrendering the limitations of its own banks that a river becomes the mighty ocean; do not be afraid to throw away the trinkets of your ego to gain the diamond of grace.

Leaving aside the abstruse theology of surrender, a simple example of surrender of the lower to the higher is physical relaxation to prepare for mental concentrations. The flesh and the spirit are often said to be in conflict. The flesh is the container, the spirit is the fluid content. Shake the container and the contents spill. Move the body and the mind loses concentration. Force the body to stay still and it rebels. Teach the body to surrender; relax your muscles and nerves; let go of them from your mind; the mind becomes free of the bondage of the flesh. This is the surrender of the body to the mind, and the mind will continue to take care of the body without catering to its every whim. This is an illustration of the progressively internal surrenders that just happen as one learns to meditate.

Would you say something of external surrender?

Gratitude and personal service. These require a curtailment of the false ego. A disciple should not think that a teaching can be purchased for a fee; not the goldmines of the entire earth are an appropriate offering for spiritual teaching, nor can you bind a teacher to any promises of grace. He will do silently or perhaps with a kick in the pants, or with a slap on the head whatever and whenever he thinks the fruit of your soul is ready and

and ripe enough to be picked. He will do it with expectation of no return, and this is the mark of a true teacher. On the other hand, the mark of a true seeker is to serve the teacher and the teaching with all mental, physical and material resources—even to produce resources where none exist, to serve as an instrument. In the Himalayas, where the disciples serve their masters for entire lifetimes, and are rewarded amply with wisdom, a person does not ask a disciple how long he has studied with the master. The disciples say, "I have washed my master's loincloth for twenty years, and then I was taught this secret." "I pressed my master's feet for thirty years before I was initiated." The spirit is immortal and the durations of eternity cannot be measured in twenty or thirty revolutions of earth.

These attitudes have a way of rubbing themselves off on true seekers in the ashrams and monasteries of yoga because there we see the masters who give their all without reserve, in utter generosity.

But start where you are and do not feel constrained to give beyond your volition. As you go deep, you will want to go deeper; as you fly upwards, you will wish to fly yet higher.

VIII
Method in Meditation

Is a method for meditation necessary? Is it not enough that one should just sit down and let the consciousness flow? Will not God's grace manifest its presence on the seeking soul without one following a method?

While it is true that higher consciousness will flow if one really invites It within, the problem, however, remains that the human personality is very much subject to the vagaries of the subconscious, which is the greatest barrier between man and the Superconscious. As one closes one's eyes and lets thoughts just flow in, all that happens is reverie and fantasies arising out of the subconscious, which the untrained mind is most likely to interpret as a divine message. This is happening now on a large scale in the name of meditation and mysticism. There is much interest in the occult and the psychic, even black magic. Much of it is nothing but dark shadows arising out of the deep murk of the subconscious, a chasing after people's insecurities. Even some of the most sublime forms of prayer and ritual, congregational worship, mass and the *puja* have become either dead forms or attempts at fulfilling mere psychological needs. That is why the occult, opium and mysticism have been lumped together in many minds.

The method taught by the great masters, who have the experience of forty centuries of initiations and practice behind them, trains the aspirant to discriminate between what arises from the subconscious and what comes down from the superconscious. It is a path of mental and spiritual purity in which no other interests come wearing the garb of spirituality.

But, wait a minute, one might say. Certainly there are true seekers ready to open their souls to God. Would they not find the higher consciousness without a method? We answer, indeed, the true aspirant will find a way. When one tells others the way, it becomes the method. Those who have truly found, show us the way. One wants to surrender completely to the inner spirit, but the flesh is weak and drags one out through the windows of the senses. How to subdue and sublimate the flesh? How to close the senses to the outside world and surrender them to the Oversoul? How to direct the emotion to become a one-pointed devotion to the spiritual path? How to keep the breath even so that it does not distract one from prayer and meditation? How to live long and healthy and conquer sloth and sleep so one has more time and energy for spiritual pursuit? How to know what is an outcome of subconscious fears and what is the experience of divine awe? What is the difference between mental depression and dark night of the soul? It is very easy to confuse the rupture of a brain cell through LSD with the manifestation of divine light in meditation. Only the guidance of the guru, through appropriate method, helps one to experience the answers to all these questions. People start meditating but the mind wanders off; how to control it? The meditation teacher tells you the way.

What is the difference between your methods and those of so many other schools? What is so special about you? How does one find out where to go? What about Zen and TM?

This has been partly answered in the first chapter. Let me reiterate that Raja Yoga is historically the first and the last yoga. The Buddhist meditation, including Zen arose out of it. The Raja Yoga word for meditation is *dhyana*, which became the Buddhist (Pali language) *jhana*, Chinese *chan* and then Japanese *zen*. The teachers who traveled to various civilizations taught these methods which were at that time already ancient. What is known to Zen is from Raja Yoga, but the converse is not true.

The phrase, *Transcendental Meditation* is redundant. Meditation, in order to be meditation, has to be transcendental. Meditation is a state that transcends the experiences of body, senses, conscious, subconscious; it transcends wakefulness, dreaming and sleep; cause, effect and sequence. This transcendental state is meditation. In the system taught under the title of TM, many claims are made for its efficacy which cannot be exclusive to it. Its proponents have taken one small drop out of a vast ocean of tradition and claimed for it the designations of an original discovery.   It is well known that in Raja Yoga, true practice of meditation begins with mantra initiation. The mantra is repeated mentally, not orally, as a continuous thought and a vibration in the mind.   This is the start of meditation.   It is not a method exclusive to an organization that has popularized it in the West.   TM is a valid method but, again, only a small part of Raja Yoga.

Various schools of meditation emphasize different methods.   It should be remembered that all the methods of meditation that have ever been taught in the history of mankind or continue to be taught this day are included in the system of Raja Yoga and are historically related to it.   There is no method that is not included in the System of Superconscious Meditation.   A particular school might teach concentration on light, or on sound, or use some other technique.   A teacher of Raja Yoga and of Superconscious Meditation is trained in all the possible methods of meditation.   Where a particular school may describe a specific method for everyone, a Raja yogi thoroughly trained in the tradition prescribes

one of many methods
to a certain depth
for a certain length of time
for a specific personality type
at a certain stage of the person's development.

Of much greater concern are the guesswork methods worked out by those who have assumed the mantle of teachers after reading a few writings on yoga;   their veracity is less than that of a science fiction novel.   We have no doubt that many readers will try to read between the lines of this book; it would be much better for their spiritual progress if they placed themselves under the discipline and learned methodically.

How long would it take me to come to spiritual realization? Are there any shortcuts? Must I go through all the disciplines?

These questions cannot be answered except with reference to the individual's background, capacity and commitment. How deep a layer of dust has he gathered around his spiritual being, and how much time does he devote to the practice? How much does he prepare himself for the more advanced practices? All of these help him to gain *adhikara*, give him the prerequisites for progress.

The method of Superconscious Meditation is a journey of the self through the self to the self. It is a process of piercing the sheaths, removing the veils of ignorance one after another and ascending the ladder of primal force—pure consciousness. It is a way of going from the relatively external, coarser to the inner and finer—from body to breath-awareness; breath to the brain and the mind; and then to the innermost spirit.

Superconscious Meditation is a unique system, known to a select group of masters. The tradition traces its record of master-disciple relationships through more than thirty-five centuries. Some of the exponents of the system were the greatest names in the Indian philosophy known as Vedanta. In the 7th and 8th centuries A.D., the system was codified by philosopher-sages like Govinda-pada and Gauda-pada and their disciple, the famous Shankaracharya. From then on, the title of Shankar-acharya has been handed down in the five major seats of the spiritual tradition. The Shankaracharyas are regarded as the supreme authority on all religious, spiritual and philosophical matters in India and Nepal. Their authority extends over many monasteries, and each monastery has kept a careful record of the master-disciple tradition.

While the intellectual philosophy of Vedanta has become relatively well known, the meditative tradition of the school of Govindapad is imparted only to a select few. Its major text, after the *Sutras* of Patanjali, is *Saundarya-lahari*, the Wave of Beauty. It sings of the waves of the Superconscious that wash the shores of human awareness. Its philosophy does not regard man as primarily a physical form but a force-field of Conscious Energy *(Chit-Shakti)*, a coil of the Serpent of Eternity *(Kundalini)* along the lines of which the body arranges itself, much as a sprink-ling of iron filings arranges itself along the lines of a magnetic field. The techniques are taught to awaken this sleeping energy of consciousness, to raise its volume and intensity so that the individual awareness becomes one with the Universal Self, which is also the force-field of the Superconscious.

In the process, one goes through intermediate stages of learning to relax, to control the body, discipline the mind, resolve emotional problems, and autogenic controls as one proceeds with the different courses.

All the aspects of the practice described in the

previous chapter are not considered absolutely necessary. The basic minimum of the practice as taught step by step is described here. One must pass through a lower course before going to a higher one.

Course One

Step 1   A.   Practice of relaxation exercises.
                   B.   Right posture. Preparatory breathing exercises; alternate breathing called "channel purification" (four types).

Step 2   Practice of breath awareness, along the lines of energy channels, in the nostrils, in the nose-bridge, in the spine.

Step 3   *Mantra* initiation. An appropriate formula of syllabic combinations is given to the initiate to repeat as a thought, not verbal sound, with breath awareness. There are specific *mantras* for different personality types, to release particular psychic energies within or to solve particular problems.
More advanced ways of using the *mantra* may be taught as the initiate progresses. The *mantra* may be changed when the full effects of the previous *mantra* have been absorbed.

From the moment of this initiation, the teacher hopes that the initiate will be able to maintain a life-long contact with the tradition so that he may be guided at every step. Many problems arise in meditation and need answers from someone experienced. Also, the initiate has to learn to discriminate between the experiences that arise from the subconscious and those arising from the superconscious, because not all internal states are eternal states. The expert's guidance will help solve the problems and to recognize valid experiences of the superconscious.

The initiate may attend lectures on philosophy, practice emotional and moral disciplines, study Sanskrit texts of the Tradition according to the oral tradition. This oral tradition is imparted only to worthy initiates, even though many inaccurate and approximate translations of a few of the texts are available in English. The disciple may choose to live in an ashram, or be advised to learn from daily life while practicing meditation and the associated disciplines.

When the disciple is considered ready, he will be led to the more advanced path, as below.

Course Two

> The meditative process may be changed. The *kundalini* is a force of the divine light and superconscious sound. The initiate may be given concentrations on
> > light
> > sound
> > one of the *chakras*, or centers of consciousness
> > the *kundalini*.

Course Three

The tradition of Superconscious Meditation depends on initiations, which means that a spark of the guru's consciousness is imparted to the disciple; it is an act of magnetizing an ordinary piece of iron by joining it to a magnet.

In the course, an initiation into a *chakra* may take place. The hidden spiritual energy is released and a blocked spiritual pathway is opened. This cannot be accomplished by anyone on his own and must be an act of grace on the part of the master.

There are many who claim to open the *chakras* and the *kundalini*. The tremendous explosion of consciousness on a cosmic scale that takes place in such initiations has to be experienced to be believed, and the power to confer such Light resides only in a few hands.

The initiation may be given by the touch of the hand, with a glance, or with a burst of mental energy.

The degree of the height and intensity of initiation depends on the disciple's ability to withstand, contain and later slowly assimilate into his nervous energy the shock of the Divine Energy. Arjuna, in the *Bhagavad-gita* (chapter XI), pleaded with the Master to withdraw the Vision, and the Old Testament (Exodus, 30:21) says, "Terrible is the face of the Lord; no one shall see it and yet live."

Course Four

Entry into the spiritual cave. Meditation as a process ends; the goal of Superconsciousness is attained. An attempt at further descriptions will violate the law of Supreme Silence.

BOOKS PUBLISHED BY THE HIMALAYAN INSTITUTE

Yoga and Psychotherapy	Swami Rama, Swami Ajaya, R. Ballentine, M.D.
Emotion to Enlightenment	Swami Rama, Swami Ajaya
Freedom from the Bondage of Karma	Swami Rama
Book of Wisdom—Ishopanishad	Swami Rama
Lectures on Yoga	Swami Rama
Life Here and Hereafter	Swami Rama
Marriage, Parenthood & Enlightenment	Swami Rama
Holistic Health	Swami Rama
Meditation in Christianity	Swami Rama, et al.
Superconscious Meditation	Pandit U. Arya, Ph.D.
Philosophy of Hatha Yoga	Pandit U. Arya, Ph.D.
Yoga Psychology	Swami Ajaya
Living with the Himalayan Masters	Swami Ajaya (ed)
Psychology East and West	Swami Ajaya (ed)
Foundations of Eastern & Western Psychology	Swami Ajaya (ed)
Meditational Therapy	Swami Ajaya (ed)
Art & Science of Meditation	L. K. Misra, Ph.D. (ed)
Swami Rama of the Himalayas	L. K. Misra, Ph.D. (ed)
Theory & Practice of Meditation	R. M. Ballentine, M.D. (ed)
Science of Breath	R. M. Ballentine, M.D. (ed)
Joints and Glands Exercises	R. M. Ballentine, M.D. (ed)
Science Studies Yoga	James Funderburk, Ph.D.
Homeopathic Remedies	Drs. Anderson, Buegel, Chernin
Hatha Yoga Manual I	Samskrti and Veda
Chants from Eternity	Institute Publication
Practical Vedanta—Selected Works of Rama Tirtha	Brandt Dayton (ed)
The Swami and Sam	Brandt Dayton
Himalayan Mountain Cookery	Mrs. R. Ballentine, Sr.
The Yoga Way Cookbook	Institute Publication